Enjoy!

REVOLUTIONIZE YOURSELF

by Cheri Swales Bair

Cheri Swales 6/19/94

This book is dedicated to...

Robby, my first-born son. Even though you lived only one day, your love lives in my heart forever.

Chris, my next son. Your personality is bigger than life. Your energy and charisma are dynamic. You brighten every room with your humor, your philosophy, and your very presence. You inspire me daily.

Marty, my youngest son. You are my rock. I know you will always be there to share a kind word and a tender hug. Your patience and support have given me the strength to face everything. You are my best friend.

*"My life was a risk
and I took it."*
Robert Frost

Copyright © 1994 by Cheri Swales Bair
All rights reserved
Success Press, 1301 Vandiver Dr., Suite 100, Columbia, MO 65202

Printed in the United States of America
First trade printing: October, 1994
10 9 8 7 6 5 4 3 2 1

Library of Congress Catalog Card Number: 94-92406

Bair, Cheri Swales
  Revolutionize Yourself.

  1. Business. 2. Self-help.

ISBN 1-878010-94-8 (pbk)

Book Design: J. Griffith
Cover Design and illustrations: Kimberlee Simmons

Contents

SECTION 3   THE INCLINATION

SECTION 4 THE MOTIVATION

Author's Note

For this book I have used the pronouns "she" and "he" interchangeably. This book is intended for men and women alike. Many of the tools I share to enhance the skill areas in the system are intended to create a form of Gender-Blending which will allow both sexes to attain the best from one another.

I have also used quotes for emphasis and tools to help you achieve your best. Sometimes an author inadvertently misquotes or credits the wrong person, or shares a technique someone else believes is theirs. I have done extensive research; however, if I have erred it is unintended.

Foreword

HOW WILL THE SUCCESS SYSTEM HELP ME?

*Success is not a magic ingredient that can be supplied
by teachers. Building on strengths allows students to
create their own success.*
-Robert Martin

As the quote says, you build on your own strengths to create success. People have a tendency to think they can go through training, read a book, or listen to tapes and magically they will become successful. They believe that all they have to do is to be like someone else, do what someone else does, to achieve success. I guarantee you, it doesn't happen that way. Success is a journey of growth, learning, failing, and regrouping. It's not just some point at which you have a certain amount of money in the bank. If you follow this system, using the tools and techniques explained, you'll achieve whatever level of success you want. BUT, you have to use the system.

As you learn the system, you'll begin to notice how the ten super powers fit together. I share with you specific tools for developing your skills in each of the ten areas. When you apply the information to your life, you'll find that the system works immediately. You'll gain a new perspective on life. You will look at everyday things differently. Your mind will open up to possibilities, and your creativity will flow. Don't judge this experience and don't stifle it. Flow with the experience and allow yourself to envelop the information and truly make it yours. I use the tools and techniques in this book everyday. I teach them to others and share them with friends and family. I truly live the system, and you will, too! As you enhance your skills in each of these ten areas, you will be able to—

- **get along with everyone you meet**

- **set and achieve goals more quickly and easily**

- **speak with power and authority**

- **creatively solve problems and develop new ideas**

- **increase your sales**

- **enhance your personal power**

SUCCESS STORIES FROM THE SYSTEM

This system empowers you to achieve whatever level of success you want and become High Performers. The results speak for themselves. Here are just a few of the successes that have been achieved by students of the High Performance Success System:

1. **A retail salesperson increased his sales by 400 percent.**

2. **A computer analyst received a book contract just two weeks after he decided he wanted to be published.**

3. **A professional architecture firm won their largest contract ever, over several larger, more favored competitors.**

4. **A woman who was so fearful of public speaking that she turned red and never made eye contact, went on to become the keynote speaker at a national convention.**

5. **A radio sales person doubled her sales, went from last to first, and maintained the top sales position until she was hired away by another radio station.**

6. **A chiropractor doubled his business.**

7. **A bank executive was promoted to VP.**

8. A college student used the tools to control stress when entering college.

9. An unemployed salesman opened his own business.

10. A woman overcame her fear and returned to college to complete her degree.

WHAT SUCCESS SYSTEM USERS SAY

Graduates of the training program and people who have listened to the tape set share their insights with me daily. Their comments about the system help me understand its tremendous value to everyone. I want to share their insights with you to help you understand what this system does for everyone who uses it.

Dave, a business consultant in Missouri, commented on the system saying, "You have to build from the ground up when you're building a structure. I think this system starts with the basic building blocks it takes for a person to be successful." He continued, "I've been through a lot of training, but never anything as focused and cohesive as this system."

Donna, a human resource specialist with a large company, stated, "There is nothing else out there like this. You can gather different bits and pieces from motivational speakers and they have their place, but this is not a motivational program; it's a life changing system. I don't think there is anything else out there like this."

Mike, entrepreneur, told me that the more skills and techniques he uses from the system, the better his life gets. He said he was in debt and couldn't make it monthly. He sat down and used idea mapping and visualization from the system and realized an additional $1200 per month! The confidence Mike gained from using the techniques from the system has enabled him to open up to his family and his friends. Talk about empowering yourself and experiencing true life enhancement!

SUCCESS FROM THE INSIDE OUT

Graduates of the training and listeners of the tape set stop me more than a year after they learn the system and tell me how they constantly catch themselves using the tools—the tools truly become part of your life. This is a key point. The system allows the information to become part of your everyday life. Because of this internalizing, you're able to use the tools consistently and move forward to success.

This is true for companies, too. I've worked with hundreds of companies that felt there was something missing from their quality improvement programs, and perhaps from their work lives in general. I found this missing piece to be the human factor. Focusing on improving quality from within each one of us individually is the key. Only then can the workplace become an empowered, highly productive place where quality thrives. This human factor is what the High Performance Success System, and this book, are all about.

SECRET PASSAGE

In this section, I want to share with you something I learned which will help all this information sink in. This secret passage is important to your understanding of the success system, and life in general. This isn't a great breakthrough or dynamic discovery. This secret passage has been talked about for years and shared with many. The reason I call it a secret passage is that most people won't "get it." These same people will read this book and a multitude of other self-help books and simply ask, "Huh?" Unfortunately, these people go through life in a daze. They are either sleepwalking or brain dead. I hope they "get it" soon.

When I worked at Honeywell, I was asleep. Asleep to the abundant knowledge in the universe and asleep to the opportunities in life. When I was in my first marriage, I was asleep. Asleep to freedom and asleep to true love and understanding. Well, it is a wonderful revelation when you finally wake up to understanding. Here's the secret passage:

Everything you need to know to get what you want in life is right inside of you.

Now you're asking, "What's so secret about that?" The secret is that most people who read this passage will never get its full mean-

4

ing. So let's look at it a little more.

Remember the Wizard of Oz? I found one of those "everything I really needed to know I learned from" excerpts, and I want to share it with you. I searched and searched and could not find the author for this; if you know who wrote it, drop me a line, so I can give proper credit in future editions.

All I Really Needed to Know, I Learned from The Wizard of Oz
Imagination can take you anywhere—even over the rainbow.
Sometimes you have to leave home to find it.
Follow the yellow brick road—but always be ready for a detour.
Faith, hope and love can work wonders, but ruby slippers can't hurt, either.
When friends stick together, they can work miracles.
Having the courage to ask for what you want is half the battle.
Hearts will never be practical until they are made unbreakable.
The grass is always greener on the other side of the rainbow.
Keep home in your heart and you can always return to it.
When you go out into the world, remember: stand up for yourself, but always be kind to the little guys.
All you need is right there inside of you.

Right here, in this simple child's story, we find the ultimate knowledge—the secret passage. We don't have to go out and find a heart, a brain, courage or success because we already have them. We have all the knowledge we need to attain whatever we want in life. All we have to do is to WAKE UP and realize it. It's not surprising that High Performance Training and this Success System have been called a near life experience.

Introduction

Today, more than ever before, it's absolutely necessary for everyone to take personal responsibility for her own success. In the training and development field we're finding that companies are not interested in investing large amounts of money in training if employees are not interested in learning and growing. Companies are getting smaller; they need employees who are high performers. Things are changing at an increased rate. If you don't accept personal responsibility for your own development, you'll be left behind. The first step in personal growth and development is making the choice to do it. This entire book is about making the right choices. I'm not interested in sharing information with you; I am interested in getting you involved with your own personal improvement. It's time to make learning a top priority like Jerry Stead, CEO of AT&T Global Information solutions. He said, "If I had one dollar left to spend, I'd spend it on education."

EMERGENCE OF THE "NEW" PROFESSIONAL

As business changes, so must we. Today's worker knows that there is no security in any job. We are better educated and more enlightened. We are demanding changes, and those changes are creating a tidal wave. Be assured that if you do not make personal changes and continue learning and growing, that tidal wave will wash you away.

It takes hard work and determination to become one of the "new" professionals. The "new" professional is thoughtful, creative, support-ive, teaming, and a risk taker. The "new" professional is in tune with everyone around him. This "new" professional is "gender-blended."

Revolutionizing yourself is absolutely necessary to fit into the new business environment. As a new professional you are a leader and a follower. You are able to transition easily amidst the chaos created by continuous change. Because of the new paradigm of business, there is a new paradigm of workers as we enter the twenty-first century. Here's a list of this change in personal thinking:

OLD THINKING	NEW THINKING
College graduate	Lifelong learner
Task oriented	Process oriented
Inward focus	Outward focus
Left brain	Whole brain
Control stress	Develop peace of mind
Change	Revolutionize
Competitive	Creative
Dollar oriented	Achievement oriented
Taking	Giving
What's in it for me?	What can I do for you?
Rigid	Flexible
Masculine	Gender blended
Power over	Empowering
Scientific	Spiritual
Control	Commune
Rational	Intuitive
Teller	Listener
Efficient—things right	Effective—right things
Goals	Planned outcomes (vision)
Motivates	Inspires
Build self-confidence	Increase self-esteem

The new professional looks at success as a lifelong adventure. You believe in falling down and getting up; you believe in learning from your failures and moving forward. You believe success is tak-ing personal responsibility for making yourself the very best you can be. And you believe in leaving the world a better place than when you entered it.

The new professional will have what's called the Janus Outlook.

8

Janus, the Roman God of Doorways, had a face on both sides of his head. This way he could see the entrance and the exit. As the emerging professional, you will find it necessary to look back in order to make tomorrow better and to project yourself into the future to make today better.

Today everyone has the ability to be successful. Everyone has a different definition of success. The High Performance Success System will help you look inside yourself and use the skills and abilities you have to move you to achieve success, whatever that success is to you. Success begins inside every person. It's just like the apple tree in this story:

> *There was a little apple tree growing in a grove of large oak trees. The little apple tree was very unhappy because it wanted to be an oak tree. The little apple tree could be heard whining, "I want to be big and tall like the mighty oak tree so I can reach the sky and touch the stars!" Soon the little apple tree blossomed and was magnificent to behold. People came for miles to see this beautiful tree. Was the apple tree satisfied? No. The apple tree cried, "I want to be big and tall like the mighty oaks. I want to reach for the sky and touch the stars!" That fall the apple tree grew big, ripe, juicy apples. People came for miles to pick the delicious fruit. Do you think the apple tree was satisfied now? Noooooo. Again the apple tree moaned, "I want to be big and tall like the mighty oak tree. I want to reach for the sky and touch the stars!" Soon a hungry little boy came by and picked an apple off the little apple tree. He pulled out his knife and instead of cutting the apple lengthwise, he cut the apple right across the middle. As he pulled the two halves apart, there, on each half where the seeds are located, were perfectly shaped stars. He showed them to the little apple tree and stated, "To touch the stars, all you have to do is look inside."*

I learned about success from the inside out over thirty years ago when I was a young girl growing up in southern Indiana. My parents never spoke of success in terms of monetary compensation or worldly possessions. They lived a life of hard, honest work and taught their children to be kind to others. My mother told me that I could do, or be, anything I wanted if I wanted it badly enough. Later I realized that success was looking back at what you had accomplished and what you had overcome to get there. Life was simple and success went to those who worked for it. And so, in Bright, Indiana, I learned to work hard and give it all I could, because success was inside of me.

I've incorporated these values into my belief system. However, today hard work alone is just not enough. Today you have to include knowing what you want, developing the skills to achieve it, and having the determination to go the extra mile, making it happen.

Today, the person who has the fortitude to take his innovative, or even crazy, idea and make it a reality is the winner. They are the risk takers. *Others can stop you temporarily; only you can do it permanently.* In using the system, you'll find that you become a risk taker. You will begin to take action naturally, on items you never did before.

This system is about revolutionizing yourself. It allows you to see many different perspectives. It helps you to accept and handle change effectively. As you experience this book and the many tools it provides, keep your eyes open for new and exciting things to begin happening. Watch closely for opportunities. With these new skills, you'll be ready for the opportunities.

CYCLE OF CHANGE

When I talk with a company about employee problems, they always discuss the massive changes that are occurring. The typical complaints I hear from companies about employees handling change include "too slow to move," "rigid thinking," "stressful," "negative," "blaming," "finger-pointing," and "confusion." The typical complaints I hear from employees about companies handling change include "too much too fast," "unreasonable," "just another program," "demanding," "stressful," and "negative." These sound pretty much the same, don't they? For employees, companies, and individuals to be successful, we all need to be able to handle change. That's why I've included in this introduction the steps you need to take in order to implement change successfully. I'll lay out for you three types of change and the five phases of implementing change successfully. These steps will help you to become flexible and adapt to change easily.

I found over the years that to make change happen successfully it must occur in five phases. This matches up with the sections of this book. This diagram shows how these phases of change occur and typically form a cycle of change.

10

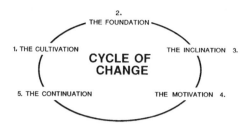

Here's an explanation of each of the five phases of change I've identified in relation to implementing individual change successfully:

1. **Cultivation.** To cultivate means to develop or foster in such a manner that something will grow. In the context of developing personal success, the cultivation means the developing of an idea or belief in an individual to assist and nurture change. This section is actually preparing you for the rest of the system. Just as the farmer cultivates his fields and prepares them to be planted, you have to prepare yourself for the change that will be occurring to enable this change to grow and flourish to move you into success.

2. **Foundation.** A foundation is the base on which something sits; it is the basis or the underlying principles on which something is built. The three powers in this section are the foundation to the system. Without developing these powers or this foundation, the system will crumble. It's just like constructing a building. Without a strong foundation the walls and ceiling cannot stand. It's your belief system. Let's face it. If you don't believe you can be successful, then you're right! This has been proven time and again with people who have won millions of dollars in the lottery. Poor when they win and soon after they win, they are poor again. We always live up to our own expectations and feelings of self-worth. If you look at Donald Trump you can see how this works also. He has a strong foundation or belief that he is worth millions of dollars. Even when he loses his wealth, he builds it up again, because of this strong foundation or belief in himself and his abilities.

3. **Inclination.** When you have a bent toward doing

11

something, then you are inclined to make it happen. The inclination is your desire to make something happen like losing weight, quitting smoking, getting organized or becoming successful. Until you identify your desires you will do little to move yourself toward these goals. The inclination section consists of the powers that uncover your desires.

4. **Motivation.** This is described as that which moves you forward. It is that internal force which moves you toward your goal. This is where you fuel the desire for which you are inclined.

5. **Continuation.** The prolonging or extension of your success. After nurturing and building to achieve success it is critical to continue it. This phase is where you identify what you must do to keep yourself at this high level of performance.

Understanding these five phases of change will help you to become a highly flexible person who will become a change master.

THREE TYPES OF CHANGE

After spending more than two decades in the business world, I believe I have run into every type of change you can imagine. For instance, at Honeywell we went from three hundred employees to over two thousand employees in just over two years. We implemented four complete computer systems in those two years. Then we laid off over seven hundred employees. Personally, I moved to three different positions in an eighteen-month period, and I had to report to six different directors in that period of time. I believe that alone is enough change to last a lifetime!

Because of the massive change that I've been through, I looked at ways to make it easier to accept. I found the first thing to help was to understand the different types of change that occur. I found three distinct types of change: planned change, unplanned change, and forced change. Here's what I mean by each.

Planned Change. A change which is known and wanted. The date and time are laid out and people are warned ahead of time that a change is being implemented. The change is worked into necessary schedules and is sometimes looked at as a necessary evil. Examples of typical planned changes include building a new building, retirement of a worker, purchasing large equipment, gaining a promotion or buying a computer system. We usually have an easier time dealing with the stress associated with planned changes. This happens because we know about them in advance, we have time to adapt, and they tend to be positive.

Unplanned Change. A change which is unknown and unscheduled. These changes are ones which happen unexpectedly. These are the changes which occur on a regular basis, some even daily, but you never know what they might be. These changes include changing meeting rooms at the last minute, temporary layoffs, car breaks down, appliances go on the fritz, child gets sick, or the boss decides to move you to another assignment at work. These changes are stressful, but usually manageable. The problem occurs when we have several unplanned changes occurring simultaneously. We tend to look at these changes as negative.

Forced Change. A change that occurs over which you have no control. These changes can be known about ahead of time or thrown at you suddenly. They can happen at any time, but are usually less frequent than the other sorts of change. Forced change would include government regulations—federal, state or local—easements enforced, death in family, divorce, victimization, or competition. These changes can occur at any time, and you might or might not know about them. These changes can be extremely stressful and sometimes seem to be unmanageable. We tend to look at these changes as negative.

You will run into all three types of change in your life. What the best scenario would be is to plan as many changes as possible and become flexible enough to handle the other two types of change. That's what I hope to do for you through this book—increase your flexibility.

At the end of several chapters, you'll find a page called the ACTION PAGE. This method is used in my Creative Leadership Course. At the end of each chapter, you decide what outcome you want to attain, what High Performance Tools you'll use to attain it, and why it is important for you to achieve this goal. I strongly encourage you to fill out the Action Page after each chapter. This will quickly help you incorporate the tools into your life. To take this a step further, you can order a package of Gold Action Cards to continue using after you've finished the book. Gold Action Cards can be taken with you, kept in a spot where you will see them frequently during the day, as a reminder to continue working on your goals using the tools. To order Gold Action Cards, see the order form in the back of this book.

As you're reading through this book, you'll be given exercises to complete. It's very important to complete these exercises as you go through each chapter. Each skill is vital to attaining the next level in the system. Take your time reading this book. Read a chapter, do the exercises, and let them soak in. Practice as you go. Make reading this book a personal evolution. By the time you're finished, you will be revolutionized.

One thing I stress over and over is—your success is up to you. I share tools in this powerful system, but if you don't use them, they won't work. It's up to you. As Aristotle said, *"Wherever I go, there I am."* You can't get away from you, so make yourself the best you can be using the information in this dynamic system. Helping others is my goal, and has been since I was a young girl in southern Indiana. I know the information in this system will move you toward your success; if you look inside yourself, you'll find it.

Happy reading!

Section 1

The Cultivation

"To cultivate means to develop or foster in such a manner that something will grow. In this context the cultivation means the developing of an idea or belief in an individual to assist and nurture change."

Chapter 1

suc cess' (sek-ses') n. a favorable termination.
sys'tem (sis'tem) n. a number of things adjusted as a connected whole; a scheme, plan, or method.

Why a Success System?

A scheme, plan or method for getting things done which provides the best use of time, energy and money.
-Anonymous

Have you ever noticed in today's society that people tend to be drawn to structure and systematic ways of doing things? For instance—

- **When I was a young girl growing up in southern Indiana, we had a telephone. I now have a telephone system with call forwarding, conference calling, smart ring and more.**

- **Once I had a toothbrush and some toothpaste; now I have a dental system which removes the plaque from my teeth and allows me to spray under my bridges and between my fillings.**

- **My mom had a potato masher; I have a food pro-**

17

**cessor that will do everything from peeling the
potato to pureeing and liquifying it!**

- **Mom applied cold cream at night to keep her skin
  looking young. I have a total facial system that
  cleanses, opens pores, exfoliates, closes pores and
  then moisturizes.**

- **I used a typewriter to type my school papers in
  high school. My children use our computer system
  to type, print, and update their essays in a third
  of the time.**

Systems are comprehensive, controllable and effective in today's
world. No matter what you do, you have probably been touched by a
system of some sort. These systems make our lives much easier and
happier. They allow us to do more in less time. We're also able to gain
better results when using a systematic approach.

This is the fundamental reason for the Success System. Success
is a very illusive term. If you ask ten people what their idea of success
is, you'll probably get ten different answers. And that's great! We're in
the age of diversity. No matter what your idea of personal success is
at any point in your life, this system will help you reach it.

A system is a set of items laid out in such a manner and connected together in such a way that they create a new whole. This new
whole allows more to happen in a very efficient manner, saving you
time and money. In this movin' and shakin' world, where we are
expected to overachieve and give 210 percent, it's no longer good
enough to learn a tool here and a technique there. We must find easier, smarter ways to move ahead and beat the competition.

I have found that highly ambitious people create systems in all
areas of their lives to make things easier and help them get through
things quicker. At work we create systems to move product through
the assembly lines, systems to control our inventory levels, and systems to monitor costs. On a personal level, we have time management
systems, financial planning systems, telephone systems, stereo sys-
tems, exercise systems, lawn care systems and even car repair sys-
tems.

We've learned that when we link items or tasks together, we
achieve greater results. An older gentleman at one of my seminars
said he read a story in a local newspaper that told about a horse
pull. The story explained how one horse was hooked up to 4,000
pounds and pulled it successfully. Another horse pulled 4,700
pounds successfully. The owners thought if they hooked the horses

together they could surely pull 9,000 pounds with no trouble at all. Indeed they did; they actually pulled 12,000 pounds! Whenever you link items or tasks together, you gain more than you do individually. The whole really is greater than the sum of its parts.

SOME PERSONAL HISTORY

When I was sixteen years old I dropped out of high school and got married, and, yes, I was pregnant. My baby was born early and didn't live. I was pregnant again within a month.

I worked and put my first husband through college. Then our relationship went sour. He abused me physically and mentally. He constantly told me I was stupid. When he got really angry he'd hit me. This went on for more than twelve years. When I couldn't take any more, I finally left and moved to Colorado.

I got busy working on a career and an education. During this time I discovered a wonderful tape set called *The Psychology of Winning* by Dennis Waitley. This was my first look at my own ignorance. It was also my first look at a wonderful future. I completed college while working at Honeywell where I met my husband, Tom. After we were married, I continued reading and searching for that one skill I needed to develop, or that one great philosophy I needed to understand to reach success. I was convinced that there was just one thing holding me back and when I discovered that one thing—"Look out, world!"

I went through training program after training program and read book after book. I started teaching courses on communication, interpersonal skills, creativity, and other topics. I found that this wasn't enough. People from my seminars were learning and gaining, but they weren't making the kind of change I hoped for. I took a long hard look at everything I was involved in, and what really worked for people and what didn't. I looked at how our environment is changing and evolving. Soon it was apparent; I had to build a system.

I began working with Chuck Sheppard and Marina Raye developing High Performance Training. I went through this extended training program and was amazed at how much more I gained—more than when I attended a typical half day training class on a single topic. I used the tools and techniques from the training and was amazed with the results. Could I be onto something? You bet. I started working harder than ever to fine tune this great discovery.

Tom and I decided to move from Colorado and test this program where no one knew us or my colleagues. We relocated to a small college town, Columbia, Missouri. In my efforts to develop a way to market and franchise this training easily, I did some mindstorming. As I was writing down the benefits from this training, I found there were consistently ten skill areas which kept appearing. I matched this information with other information I found on success. I also looked at all our graduates and found that the truly successful ones had developed all ten of these skill areas. YES! Finally, a system in which individuals could learn and thrive, and attain success.

I was so excited about this dynamic system that all I wanted to do was market The High Performance Training Course, getting this information out to as many people as possible. Returning from a trip, I was reading *USA Today* and noticed a classified ad: Products Needed for Infomercials. I decided to create an audio tape set based on the training program and sell it on a national infomercial, an ideal way to spread this new system to as many people as possible. I refined and organized the system, and after months the model was finally pulled together on the marker board in my training room. Hence, The High Performance Success System: Ten Super Powers of Achievement.

THE HIGH PERFORMANCE PRINCIPLES

The system includes twenty High Performance Principles. Research has shown that High Performers have a special mind-set that guides their decisions and actions. I have brought this mind-set together into the Twenty High Performance Principles. This book will help you adopt them as part of your mind-set. As you read through them, think of ways they can make a powerful difference in your life.

1. Dream BIG dreams. It's important to stretch our vision and reach for that really big dream. High Performers always go for the job, the contract, or the idea that is just a little out of reach.

When I do career counselling with clients, the first thing I ask them is how much they want to earn. I asked this of one client, Dave. He said he wanted to make $20,000 per year because this was more than he was now earning. After we completed the session, he said he wanted to earn at least $50,000 per year and run his own business. Within one year, he left his job and went into partnership running a cleaning business. Dave had never done any of this before and when he started looking bigger, he found his dream.

High Performers don't set goals that are easily attainable, they push themselves to reach for the stars. So make sure that you dream BIG dreams.

2. Do what you love to do. Ninety percent of us don't know what we want to be when we grow up! Ask yourself what you love to do and then just do it. When you do what you love, prosperity will follow.

Another graduate took this to heart. Mary worked for a Fortune 500 firm for over ten years. When they offered large bonuses to take a layoff, she jumped at the opportunity. With her funds she started a photography business. This had been her passion for years, but she was afraid to take the leap. When faced with a decision, she chose to do what she loves to do and is now quite happy.

3. Focus on your unique strengths. What makes you unique? How are you different? Sometimes our unique strength is our biggest weakness. Focus on the items that are uniquely yours, and success will follow you wherever you go.

A cleaning lady heard this principle and decided to focus on her biggest weakness—her appearance. She was quite ugly. She also had quite a sense of humor. Focusing on her weakness, appearance, and her strength, humor, she went on to become a household name—Phyllis Diller.

Maybe you have a unique weakness or a negative feature or attribute. What is there about it that you can turn into a positive?

4. Think of yourself as self-employed. In today's world of mergers, acquisitions and take-overs, there is no perceived "security" as we assumed for many years. Now, more than ever before, we must make ourselves the best we can be, no matter where we work or what we do. After all, you are the only security you have!

This became apparent to many employees of Honeywell. As this large corporation made the decision to leave the mainframe computer market, many of their employees were left homeless. Many of my co-workers who were let go couldn't get over the shock that their security was gone. Many of them had been with the company for more than fifteen years. Many of them took lesser jobs just to regain that feeling of security. When my husband left Honeywell, he decided to become part of many companies. He now consults with start-up companies. He helps them to set up their organization and bring customers on. He takes a piece of the company in lieu of a large salary. When the company becomes successful he reaps the benefits.

No matter who you report to, you must think of yourself as, YOU, Inc. When you are able to think of yourself as self-employed, you'll do better on your current job and in any subsequent positions you hold.

5. Never consider the possibility of failure.
Scientists tell us that the bumble bee should not be able to fly because of the small size of its wings in comparison to its large body. But, the bumble bee doesn't know this. It doesn't consider the possibility of failure—it just flies! We have to be like the bumble bee, and never consider failure as an option.

Colonel Sanders was turned down repeatedly as he attempted to market his chicken recipe. Thomas Edison failed to invent the light bulb over and over again. Abraham Lincoln lost many political races and had a nervous breakdown before he became President. Walt Disney filed bankruptcy four times before he was able to make his dream a reality. I failed in two businesses I started before I opened my training/consulting firm.

Do not look at failure as an option. Every failure is merely a milestone in your success journey. NEVER think failure...only results!

6. Develop a clear set of goals for a solid life plan. Research has proven time and again that people who have clear, written goals achieve far more than those who do not. Like the old saying, "If you fail to plan, you plan to fail."

I spent the first thirty years of my life setting goals. But I never wrote them down. Everything was in my head. I did achieve many of my goals, but I realized after I started using written plans that I would have achieved the others much quicker and easier if they had also been written and clearly stated.

Write out your goals and keep them in a spot where you will see them frequently. Write out short term as well as long-term goals. One of my clients did this and ended up getting married even sooner than she had written down.

7. Work hard and work smart. Eight hours of work per day is merely survival. As High Performers, we go the extra mile, and we make sure we're doing things the easiest and fastest way possible without compromising quality.

This was an essential quality in employees at Honeywell. The employees who put in at least twelve hours each day were the ones who were promoted and given the visible assignments. The twelve hours didn't have to be on the job. The time could be spent attending classes or professional meetings. While I worked more than forty hours per week at Honeywell, I also attended evening and weekend classes to complete my degree.

These workers spent more time working than socializing. They found a way to complete every assignment. If they ran into a roadblock, they searched until they were able to find a way around or over it. This is where I learned a very valuable lesson: It is much easier to gain forgiveness than to gain permission. This philosophy helped me expedite many programs.

23

8. Associate with positive High Performers. The most effective way to be a High Performer is to be around others who are High Performers. No matter where you are or what you do, identify the people who are centers of influence—the ones who set policy, make decisions, influence decisions, hire, fire, or have high personal power. These are the individuals who will advance your career and increase your sales. If you want to soar like an eagle, you can't hang around turkeys!

9. Remain teachable all of your life. It has been said that when we stop growing, we begin dying. High Performers are always open to new ideas, attending seminars, reading books, listening to tapes, and learning everything they can.

I admire people who believe in continuous learning. My colleague, Muriel, who has achieved much greatness in our community made this statement when she signed up for our leadership training: "I was wondering what I would do this summer to improve myself."

The number one reason people sign up to participate in training is to learn something new. My clients range in age from sixteen to sixty-nine. Cal, the sixty-nine year old, said he wanted to become less cynical and to attain his goals. He is still setting goals at sixty-nine!

10. Start by knowing you are already there. High Performers are able to project themselves into their vision as if they have already achieved it. Steven Covey in his book, *The Seven Habits of Highly Effective People*, says, "Begin with the end in mind."

In planning production and in planning my life, I always started with my end result. Ask yourself, "What do I want to accomplish?" Lay out your plan from there! When my grandmother planted her garden each year, she didn't just plant some seeds. She planned out what she wanted to have in her pantry in December. Then she decided what to plant. We have to do the same thing in planning our career and our lives.

11. Develop hardiness and be able to bounce back. Stress, worry, negativity, pressure and all the other things that happen to us daily are merely energizers for High Performers. We use them to our advantage, just like the man who can put things behind him or the woman who just lets things roll off her back. High Performers are hardy people who take care of themselves so they are prepared for anything.

Hard work is good for you, but it brings with it a lot of stress and negativity. To become a High Performer you must develop hardiness. When Donald Trump lost millions you didn't see him wringing his hands and pacing the floor. He has developed hardiness and is able to take things in stride and bounce back to regain his fortune.

Practice good stress reduction techniques and develop a network of friends. These are the two main ingredients to hardiness.

12. Unleash your natural creativity. According to Rudolph Flesch, "Creative thinking may mean simply the realization that there's no particular virtue in doing things the way they have always been done." Creativity is using more of our senses and becoming more aware of opportunities and ideas.

As a "new professional," you will find that this is a critical step. Competition breeds stress and anxiety. It's time we forget competing and begin creating. Understand that the universe provides plenty for everyone; we simply need to be creative and develop ways to grab our share. This became very apparent to me when I met Les and Carolyn, two individuals who had decided the traditional job market would not help them attain their goals. They became active in network marketing. Instead of trying to work hard and outsell the other network marketers, they took the creative approach. They looked at their product to determine who would find it appealing. They approached individuals who were good at marketing and brought them into their group. After six months they had more than four hundred people in their down line.

13. Be an unshakable optimist. Attitudinize! Strike a positive mental attitude. Refuse to look at the negative, avoid the complainer, never whine, and above all else, smile! I have met many positive people, but the one who stands out to me is Ann. I have never heard her say anything negative about anyone. She is always in a good mood. Her smile lights up a room. Ann recently had a son. I am convinced he will have a wonderful life because his mother will teach him to attitudinize.

14. Develop a reputation for speed and dependability. When I worked for Honeywell we had a policy when we were promoting someone. If they had a sense of urgency, they were promotable.

This is true among business owners. As a member of a Chamber of Commerce, I've found it's easy to spot the business owners who have good follow-through and who are dependable. In all of my customer service training, this helps companies to stand out immediately. When people know you take action and can be relied upon, you are considered a High Performer.

15. Be honest with yourself and others. There are no degrees of honesty; either you are or you aren't. When you cannot be honest with yourself, it's not possible to be honest with others.

I find this to be a severe problem in business today. The level of ethical behavior has deteriorated to the point of becoming criminal. My husband Tom worked for a boss who was covering up over expenditures and gross errors. Tom couldn't tolerate this type of behavior, so he resigned after meeting with his boss and his boss' boss. Tom was true to himself and his beliefs. Because of this attribute he is able to develop trust almost immediately.

16. Develop decisiveness. Make a decision. Enough said.

17. Concentrate single-mindedly on one thing at a time. When you are able to focus on one thing at a time, it is sure to get completed. When we are fragmented, we lose control and accomplish nothing.

This is difficult for women. I know! I can't walk from my desk to the restroom without completing four tasks on the way. My desk is filled with projects on which I'm working. I have to force myself to focus on one thing in order to complete it. While I was working on this book, I had to let other projects go.

Men have no problem with this principle because it is part of their makeup. Tom can't do more than one thing a time. If he is told three items or interrupted in the middle of a task he loses his concentration and effectiveness. Because of his ability to focus, he is able to gain constant results. He increased the sales of my training company by remaining focused on sales. We went from two classes per year to eleven classes per year.

18. Be persistent and determined. Never, never, never give up. The average sale takes five to six contacts before it is closed. Saint Catherine of Siena said "Nothing great was ever done without much enduring."

19. Discipline yourself. We are usually our own worst critics. Instead of having a critic, turn yourself into a coach. This coach can help you create the discipline you need to accomplish many things.

20. Teach everyone you meet the High Performance tools. Whenever you teach someone else, you learn and understand the concepts yourself. Teach everyone you meet the tools and principles from this system and they will become part of your life.

These principles are used by successful people everywhere. Brian Tracy reminds us of this when he says, "Success is not an accident. Success comes as the result of practicing proven methods. If you do what other successful people do, in almost any field, you will be successful too!" There is no need to reinvent the wheel. Simply incorporate these attributes into your life and you too will be successful.

High Performance Training has been called a near life experience. Through the proven techniques in this system, you will be developing an owner's manual for your brain. You will be given tools which are powerful. I encourage you to use them with the utmost integrity and always go for a win/win conclusion.

As you experience this book, look for the options and opportunities. You will be gaining a personal diversification as you go through your own personal revolution. Get ready to learn the ten key components on which High Performers rate consistently superior; and how you can increase your abilities in these areas by thirty to fifty percent or more.

Here are some tips to help you gain the most from this book:

1. **Read actively and with an open mind.** Some ideas may seem overstated; however, research shows most people filter out much of what they read.

2. **Make notes for yourself and refer to them frequently.** Write down specific comments that especially mean something to you so you'll be able to remember them later.

3. **When necessary, stop reading and complete specific exercises, especially those at the end of the chapters.** Use this hands-on experience to reinforce your learning.

4. **Start using the techniques immediately.** Research shows that if you don't use a new application within twenty-four to forty-eight hours, you probably never will.

5. **Teach the techniques to friends, family, and coworkers.** As you teach the tools and techniques to others, it reinforces them in your mind and helps them to become a part of your everyday life.

This book is filled with tools, techniques, and tips in each of the ten skill areas which will help you attract success. I have packed this book with ideas from people who have attended my seminars and training programs. All of these tools and tips are intended to assist you, not in and of itself make you successful. Choose the ones that work best for you and use them religiously. If a tool isn't right for you, forget about it or revise it to work best for you. The more tools you use, the quicker you will see results.

In order for you to gain the most from this valuable information, you need to remember something very important. I want to share this with you in a special story that I use to close our first session of the High Performance Training—Creative Leadership Course:

> *There was a young boy who was about to enter kindergarten. He wanted to do a good job, so he asked his father what he should do. His father replied, "It's simple. Do whatever the teaches asks, work as hard as you can, give it all you've got—AND THEN SOME!" The little boy did quite well. He went on through grade school and high school and as he entered college he went back to his father and asked again what he should do to be highly successful in college. His father replied, "It's simple. Do whatever the teachers ask, work as hard as you can, give it all you've got—AND THEN SOME!" After college the young man got married and as they were having their first child he went back to his father and asked how he could be a really good father. His father replied, "It's simple. Do the right things, work as hard as you can, give it all you've got—AND THEN SOME!" Several years later, his little boy was entering kinder- garten. The little boy wanted to do a good job so he went to his father and asked what he should do. This man remembered what his father had said to him and he looked at his little boy and smiled as he replied, "It's simple. Do whatever the teachers ask, work as hard as you can, give it all you've got—AND THEN SOME!"*

As this story so beautifully points out, success comes to those who really put out the effort. I challenge each of you to use all of the techniques in this book, work as hard as you can, give it all you've got—AND THEN SOME!

Chapter 2

Mind/Brain Technologies

*"Brain, n. An apparatus with which we think
that we think"*
-Ambrose Bierce

Many of the tools I share in this book are based on theories and/or technologies that have been developed from studies of the human brain. It's important to provide a basic overview of these technologies for anyone who may not be familiar with them. Specifically I will be covering the following mind/brain technologies: Right Brain/Left Brain Theory; Neurolinguistic Programming; Educational Kinesiology; Psycholinguistics, Geometric Psychology; and Non-verbal Communication.

I am not going to provide great detail regarding the technologies. I'm simply going to share an overview and definition of each to help you understand the concepts. The tools and techniques I share will be the easiest and simplest for you to learn and use. I have found that when a technique is too complicated and too complex, people won't use it. No matter how good the technique, if you aren't using it, it won't help you!

Because of the makeup of the two genders, these technologies are extremely important to understand. Here is where "gender-blending" comes in. I write about developing whole brain tendencies versus using only one side of the brain predominately. "Gender-blending" is more than just picking up a few traits from the opposite sex. It's actually developing and consciously using more of your brain power—your whole brain. By using the whole brain you are able to become more focused yet rid yourself of mental rigidity. You become highly flexible and handle change with ease. You increase your power and authority, and get in tune with your intuition and feelings. It is the best of both worlds.

We hear a lot of talk today about the differences between the sexes. These differences don't have to hold us back, for they are at the core of professional success for both genders.

RIGHT BRAIN/LEFT BRAIN

Thanks to the work of people like Roger Sperry in the 60's and 70's, we know that we have two distinct hemispheres to our brains. These two sides provide us with two distinct types of mental activity. Here's a diagram to help you understand the distinctions between the two sides:

Right Brain	**Left Brain**
(Intuitive Brain)	(Try Brain)
Emotional	Logical
Nonverbal	Verbal
Spontaneous	Rational
Creative	Structured
Nonjudgmental	Judgmental
Lateral Thinking	Linear Thinking
Big Picture	Little Picture
Abstract	Concrete
Controls Left Body	Controls Right Body

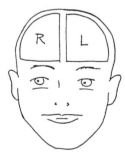

More recent research has shown us that in fact we have four distinct quadrants to our brain and each operates different functions. For our purposes we only need to focus on the two hemisphere information.

One of the main differences between men and women is the natural tendency to different brain dominances. Men have a tendency to be more left-brained and women have a tendency to be more right-brained. This isn't just a learned habit. It happens shortly after conception. A hormone washes over the brain of the male fetus and seals off some access to the right hemisphere. The *corpus callosum*, the fibers connecting the two sides of the brain, in a woman are larger than those of men. Regardless of this natural difference, we can still develop the side of the brain which is less dominant by exercising our minds—it's like brain aerobics.

Research involving some of our great thinkers such as Einstein help us to understand how important it is to develop both sides of our brain. According to the diagram, you would naturally think that Einstein, the brilliant mathematician, would be left-brained. Research showed that he loved mind games and music and was whole brained. Likewise, the great painter Picasso would appear to be right-brained as an artist. Yet he was organized and logical in his routine and decision making; therefore, whole-brained.

My husband Tom is without a doubt Mr. Left Brain. He can focus on only one thing at a time. Otherwise he becomes overwhelmed. He doesn't understand, nor is he comfortable with emotions. Everything must have logic behind it, or it is incorrect or invalid to him. He tends to be rigid in his movements, not rhythmic. He is task oriented and somewhat inflexible. I, on the other hand, do at least five things at a time constantly. Emotion is my middle name. I use logic for all my decisions—just a different type of logic than Tom's. It is very difficult for me to focus on one thing at a time; therefore I tend to overwhelm myself with too much of everything.

You'll notice the difference in the extreme left-brained individual and the extreme right-brained individual almost instantly. The left brainer will operate as follows:

- **Balances checkbook to the penny**
- **Usually skeptical of new ideas**
- **Organizes closet by color or size**
- **Inflexible toward change**
- **Not very talkative**
- **Enjoys logic and problem solving**
- **Buys only after research into the best value**
- **Doesn't appear friendly**
- **Analyzes everything completely**
- **Typically serious**
- **Always wants more information**

- Argues through logic, not emotion
- Very systematic in his routine
- Uses concrete v. abstract statements
- Doesn't like mistakes
- Leans toward boring

The right-brained person will operate quite differently:

- Rarely balances checkbook
- Open to new ideas
- Unorganized and messy
- Flexible to change
- Very open and talkative
- Uses intuition in problem solving
- Buys presents for others that she wants
- Friendly and caring
- Buys on emotion
- Typically fun-loving
- Accepts little information
- Argues through emotion v. logic
- Spontaneous
- Uses abstract v. concrete statements
- Takes mistakes in stride
- Colorful personality

It is also important to understand that the right side of the brain controls the left side of the body and the left side of the brain controls the right side of the body. So, left-handed people are the only ones in their right mind! (Sorry, I couldn't resist!)

Our brains are wondrous. But we don't understand its functions completely, nor do we exercise it enough. We have been told that we use less than one percent of our brain's power and only a little of its capacity. We have much to learn about the brain, but one thing is sure: we all need to use our brain more. Use this list to help you understand the characteristics of the two hemispheres.

Left Mode and Right Mode
Characteristics of the Brain

LEFT MODE

Verbal: using words to name, describe, define

Analytic: Figuring things out step-by-step and part-by-part.

Concrete: relating to things as they are, at the present moment.

Analogic: seeing likenesses between things, understanding metaphoric relationships.

Temporal: keeping track of time, sequencing one thing after another.

Rational: drawing conclusions based on facts.

Digital: using numbers, as in counting.

Logical: drawing conclusions based on logic one thing following another in order.

Linear: thinking in terms of linked ideas, one thought directly following another.

RIGHT MODE

Nonverbal: awareness of things, but minimal connection with words.

Synthetic: Putting things together to form wholes.

Symbolic: Using a symbol to stand for something. Example: + stands for adding.

Abstract: taking a small bit of information and using it to represent the whole thing.

Nontemporal: without a sense of time.

Nonrational: not requiring a basis of facts; willingness to suspend judgment.

Spatial: Seeing where things are in relation to other things, and how parts go together to form a whole.

Intuitive: making leaps of insight, often based on incomplete patterns, feelings or visual images.

Holistic: seeing whole things all at once; perceiving overall patterns.

NEUROLINGUISTIC PROGRAMMING (NLP)

NLP has been called the software for our brains. It is considered the communication that we have with ourselves and with others. Conceived and developed by Richard Bandler and John Grinder many years ago, NLP has been the subject of much controversy and much popularity. For the purposes of this book, I want to describe the very basics of NLP. I am not a psychologist, nor am I a neurologist. I am a specialist in human resources who has found a technology which is beneficial to professionals. In this book I'll share basic techniques which can be used simply and easily.

I will discuss the three sensory modalities through which we learn and communicate on a daily basis. We all have each of these modes; however, we tend to be dominant in one area. The three distinct styles are visual, auditory, and kinesthetic. Here's what is meant by these three styles:

Visual: pictures, scenes, images

Auditory: sounds, hearing, tones

Kinesthetic: feelings, senses, touch

I refer to the way that we take in information and communicate with others as VAK. I will refer to VAK throughout this book.

Also, from NLP, I will share some techniques to help you change old feelings, establish rapport with anyone, and access "states of excellence."

EDUCATIONAL KINESIOLOGY (EK)

EK was developed by Dr. Paul Dennison and his wife Gail. It was originally developed for dyslexic children to help them read easier. This technology comes from right brain/left brain theory. EK tells us that we have an imaginary mid-line which runs down the front of our bodies. When we cross this mid-line, we create electrochemical impulses which "switch-on" the whole brain.

As a society we have a tendency to be homolateral. We tend to operate out of one side of our brain. Typically in business this is the left brain. You know, "Get down to business, the bottom line." Using exercises from EK, we can "switch-on" the whole brain and become less stressed and more productive. This allows us to become more creative and effective on the job.

Keep in mind that the exercises I share in this book are exercises from EK, developed for children. Many of the exercises have names aimed at children. Business professionals who resist this valuable information because it makes them feel uncomfortable are missing a valuable opportunity to expand their abilities. If you never feel uncomfortable, then you aren't changing and growing. When you begin to feel uncomfortable, just know that the feeling will eventually pass and you'll reach a new level of understanding or enlightenment and become a more effective person.

PSYCHOLINGUISTICS

In this technology you will learn to understand the psychological meaning of words we use. Many of the words that we use on a daily basis have hidden meanings or mental meanings placed on them by the listener. Many of these meanings are subliminal and only known at the subconscious level. When we understand the "other" meaning given to the words we use, we begin to understand why people react to us in a certain way, or why we never seem to communicate effectively with people.

Again, I want to stress that I don't go into technical aspects of psycholinguistics or other technologies in this book. I take simple tools and techniques and share them in a manner easily understood and applied.

GEOMETRIC PSYCHOLOGY

This technology is also taken from right-brain/left-brain theory. Much of this theory has been used by trainers and speakers for years. Dr. Susan Delinger researched and wrote about this theory in her book, *Psycho Geometrics*. In the book she identifies five personality types associated with five geometric shapes. The theory is that based on our brain dominance; we're drawn to different forms and shapes in our environment. We reflect those shapes in our personality in how we interact with others, how we do our jobs, and the items we purchase.

NON-VERBAL COMMUNICATION

This technology is powerful when understood. Only seven percent of our communication is in the words we speak. The other ninety-three percent is non-verbal. As men and women, we use different and distinct non-verbal cues to communicate, largely because of our brain dominance. When you look at these movements and understand them, you can begin to understand why "gender-blending" is so powerful. I particularly encourage "gender-blending" in your non-verbal communication skills.

Non-verbal communication has been broken down into six specific areas according to Paul R. Trimm, in his book on managerial communication:

1. **Kinesic.** Gestures, body movements, facial expressions.

2. **Proxemics.** Personal use of physical space.

3. **Paralanguage.** Voice qualities, tonality, rate of speed, laughing, yawning.

4. **Olfaction.** Sense of smell.

5. **Tactile.** Skin sensitivity, stroking, hitting, touching.

6. **Artifacts.** Clothes, glasses, height, weight, skin color, general appearance.

I will explain these in greater detail later. I'm not talking simply about body language with non-verbal communication. I am talking about the meanings we add to our words by the way we move, dress, stand, speak, smell, touch, and the personal space we take. All these areas have special meaning in the business world. In order to develop personal power, it is critical to understand exactly what we are saying at all levels, with or without "words."

All these technologies have been used in the success system because of their unique similarity—they are all associated with your brain/computer. All these technologies are powerful when used properly. Many people have said that NLP can be manipulative. They're right. I encourage you to use all these tools with the utmost integrity, always working towards a win/win conclusion.

Chapter 3

The High Performance Success System: Ten Super Powers of Achievement

*High Performers continuously get the most out of life.
My goal in offering this system is to help you revolu-
tionize yourself so you can achieve your
highest performance, personally and professionally.
Use this system—it works!*
Cheri Swales Bair

High Performance Training was developed several years ago and has evolved into a dynamic model for success. When you apply this model, you'll find it works.

The High Performance Success System is the result of continuous, in-depth research into the understanding of human excellence. I'll identify the ten elements of successful people and show how these elements build one on another. This building creates a synergistic effect within each person, which in turn, empowers you to continuous high performance in all areas of your life.

TEN SUPER POWERS OF ACHIEVEMENT

I will refer to each of the ten areas or elements as powers. The first power in the High Performance Model is **Self-Esteem—The Foundation of Success.** Self-esteem is critical to your success as High Performers. When we know how to develop self-esteem, we're in control of feeling good about who we are and what we do. High self-esteem helps us gain the confidence and courage to achieve a constant level of high performance.

The second power in the success model is **Communication—The Ultimate Advantage.** As we move into the twenty-first century, communicating with real understanding is absolutely essential. In the Success System, we first develop self-esteem so that we are better able to increase communication skills. This enables us to inspire others to take action, the purpose behind much of our communications. It doesn't matter with whom you're dealing, the techniques in The High Performance Success System will enable you to respond and communicate effectively.

The third power is **Human Relation Skills**—or, as I call it, **The Human Factor.** It's nearly impossible to develop good human relation skills if you have low self-esteem and poor communication skills. People skills. We hear it all the time. No matter how automated the world becomes, we always work through people. We still have relationships with people. I'll show you ways to transform your relationships quickly.

Power number four is **Positive Attitude—A Personal Empowerment Model.** It's been said you cannot climb uphill by thinking downhill thoughts. All High Performers are "can-do" people. They are empowered through a positive attitude to take positive action.

The fifth power is **Peace of Mind—the High Performance State.** High Performers are aware of their stress and use it to their advantage. As a High Performer you'll learn to control your reaction to stressful situations accessing true peace of mind.

Power six is **Personal Balance—Controlling Your World.** High performance people are equally in tune with their personal lives as well as their professional lives. They understand the connection of mind, body and spirit, working to nurture all three areas as a whole.

Power seven is **Creativity—The Whole Brain Adventure.** Innovation and creativity are essentials to the High Performer. You'll learn to use your whole brain, tapping into the resources of the right hemisphere. You'll understand how to switch-on both sides of the brain to release tension and generate new and interesting ideas.

The eighth power is **The Ten Realms of Outcome Planning.** Most

of us have goals, but we don't always reach those go&
ever, always have an outcome. High Performers simpl
comes in advance. As a High Performer, you'll l
method for outcome planning and understand how im
develop your core desires.

Power nine is **Passion—The Propelling Force.** My favorite autho₁,
Anonymous, once said, "Those who have no fire in themselves, cannot warm others." High Performers have a deep, intense passion for
life and it shows in everything they do.

The tenth power is **Action-Orientation—The Catalyst to High
Performance.** Thomas Huxley said, "The great aim of life is not
knowledge but action." High Performers make things happen. With
the synergy created by developing the other nine elements in this
model, you naturally become an action-oriented person.

UNIVERSAL INSIGHTS

I'm going to take you on a journey through this system, one power
at a time. The rest of this book focuses on the individual powers and
provides you with real tools to help you become your most effective
and productive. In order to achieve success and use this system properly, you must first understand some very basic universal insights.
I've gathered these universal insights from my favorite authors and
trainers. You may have heard some of them before. I think they merit
repeating.

- **Life is our mirror, whatever we give out is exactly what we receive in return.**

- **Whatever we think about is what we become.**

- **The past does not equal the future.**

- **There is no such thing as failure, only results.**

- **When you do what you love to do, money will follow.**

- **As you help others achieve their goals, you will prosper greatly.**

- **When you are ready to learn, a teacher will appear.**

- **Whatever we resist, persists.**

- **Whenever life events are repeated, you have a lesson to learn.**

- **Everyone's perception is right.**

- **Your ability to relax is in direct proportion to your ability to trust life.**

- **Life is a journey, not a destination.**

- **As your awareness increases, your reality expands.**

- **When one door closes, another opens.**

- **Everything in life happens for a reason.**

- **You are the only teacher you'll ever need.**

Incorporate these universal insights into your thought pattern. Think about them and reflect on your life. These insights are important to your success. Until you believe and understand these truths, you will struggle with the rest of the Success System.

Section 2

The Foundation

"A foundation is the base on which something rests; it is the basis or the underlying principles on which something is built. The three powers in this section are the basis for the system. Without them your system will crumble."

Chapter 4

Self-Esteem: The Foundation of Success

Of all the judgments that we pass in life, none is as important as the one we pass on ourselves, for that judgment touches the very center of our existence.
Nathaniel Branden

Over the past several years, self-esteem has risen to the forefront of our minds. It has become so important that the state of California developed a task force to address the issues surrounding self-esteem. They spent three years researching and investigating these issues. *Appreciating my own worth and importance and having the character to be accountable for myself and to act responsibly toward others.* This is the definition of self-esteem as stated by the California Task Force to Promote Self-Esteem and Personal and Social Responsibility.

Virginia Satir, a well-known family therapist, was a pioneer behind this group. She addressed the concept of self-esteem and created new therapies as a result. Because of her work and the work of many others, we have reached a level of understanding about self-esteem that helps us to develop it in ourselves and in others.

I find self-esteem to be the single most important aspect in developing any individual or company. Building self-esteem is the foundation for the High Performance Success System. As we build and nurture our self-esteem, we are able to add the other skills which create a synergistic effect for continuous High Performance.

WHY IS SELF-ESTEEM THE FOUNDATION TO SUCCESS?

Why is self-esteem so important to your success? Because your self-esteem affects the way you live your life. It affects how you think, how you feel, and how you act toward yourself and others. I equate self-esteem with personal dignity. After more than twelve years with my ex-husband abusing me, mentally and physically, he moved out on the same day that I was permanently laid off from my job. I sat down that evening and cried. My tears came from two aspects of that devastating day. First, I was fearful of being without a job, and second, I was relieved that my horrible marriage was finally over. I was so angry that I sat down and wrote a poem. I think this poem says a good deal about personal dignity and self-esteem no matter who you are.

Dignity

You took my youth...and made me old;
You took my warmth...and left me cold.

You took my heart...and gave me pain;
You took my sun...and made it rain.

You took my purity...and left me used;
You took my pride...and left it bruised.

You took my smile...and made me frown;
You took my trust...and let me down.

You took my hopes...and refused to try;
You took my honesty...and made me lie.

You took my love...and made me weep;
You won't take my dignity...it's mine to keep.

It's been said that there are no victims, only volunteers. When you allow another person to take advantage of you, you are volunteering. It's up to you to make sure you are not a victim (caused by low self-esteem and lack of assertiveness). The following story about a minister stresses this point.

A minister was caught in a flood in his small church building. Rain continued to fall and the water contin-

ued to rise. A man from the congregation came by in a small boat and told the minister to get in because everyone was evacuating. The minister replied, "No thanks, I'm staying with the church building." A little later another boat came by and requested that the minister get aboard. By now the water had risen to the second floor of the church. Still the minister replied, "No, I am going to stay with the church." The water continued to rise and soon the minister had to climb to the top of the steeple. A helicopter came by and dropped a ladder. The minister said, "No, I'm loyal and I'm staying with the church. I know God will save me." The water continued to rise and the minister drowned. When he got to heaven he was angry because God hadn't saved him. When he approached God and asked, "How could you let this happen? I was your most loyal servant." God replied, "What did you expect? I sent two boats and a helicopter!"

We have to realize it's up to us to get out of the volunteering and into succeeding. I was fortunate growing up because I had good parents who helped develop a deeply seeded feeling of self-worth in me. They spent time with me and we had a good line of communication. This helped me feel good about myself. Over time it added to my belief system that I was a good person, no matter what anyone else said or did, even when I made a mistake. Because of this strong foundation of self-esteem, even though my self-confidence was shattered by my bad marriage, I was able to move forward and establish a new relationship, new jobs, my own company, and my own success.

When you have high self-esteem you will accomplish more. You'll have more loving relationships. You'll treat others in a more positive manner. When you have low self-esteem, you will be less effective, achieve less, become less lovable, and treat others poorly. Therefore, it's clear to see why our self-esteem is so critical to the other nine skill areas. Without self-esteem we have no support, no foundation on which to build.

HOW DO I KNOW IF I HAVE LOW SELF-ESTEEM?

There are specific characteristics of low self-esteem people and high self-esteem people. When you understand these characteristics you will be able to identify if you are suffering from low self-esteem. You will also be able to identify others around you.

HIGH SELF-ESTEEM PERSON

1. Handles change easier and is more flexible.
2. Open and caring to others.
3. Enthusiastic, happy, full of energy and a zest for life.
4. Believes herself to be equal to others.
5. Makes decisions and acts upon them.
6. Has strong values.
7. Enjoys self and doing things alone.
8. Takes responsibility when he makes a mistake.
9. Enjoys competition.
10. Outgoing and fun.

LOW SELF-ESTEEM PERSON

1. Inflexible and reluctant to change.
2. Shut off from others and inwardly focused.
3. Bad attitude and negative.
4. Feels inferior to others.
5. Avoids making decisions and problem solving.
6. Blames others and is overly critical.
7. Sometimes feels persecuted.
8. Dislikes competition.
9. Timid or shy.
10. Very sensitive to criticism.

There are more characteristics, but I think you can determine from these where you fall. Sometimes we jump from high to low self-esteem, depending on the circumstances.

DEVELOPING SELF-ESTEEM

We are born with no concept of self-worth or self-esteem. This is developed in each of us over time. Unfortunately, instead of developing and nurturing our self-esteem, we slowly have it chipped, and eroded away. We are told "NO" more than 35,000 times before we go to kindergarten. Even worse, it all goes down hill from there! Remember a time as a child when you were told something critical about yourself such as: "You're so slow," "Stand up straight," "You'll never amount to anything," "Why can't you be more like your brother?" "You're ugly," "You're fat." "You're skinny," and so on.

Every time you heard this type of critical statement, you checked to see if there might be some truth to it. If you had any doubts, you accepted it. Over time, it became reality. We carry these beliefs about our self-worth into our schools, jobs, and relationships. And, if things aren't good in these places, our self-esteem gets nibbled at even more.

It takes several years for your self-esteem to be lowered, and it will take time to turn it around. The good news is that it can be done! It's all a matter of choice. We can choose to look down on ourselves or to respect ourselves. I was told a story by my good friend and mentor, Chuck Sheppard, that helped me understand the concept of choice.

> *There were several workers who finished up their mornings work and went to lunch. As they opened their lunch pails, one worker became very upset. "Oh, no! Not a peanut butter and jelly sandwich again! It's always peanut butter and jelly, I can't stand it any longer." One of the other workers said, "Calm down! All you have to do is tell your wife not to pack any more peanut butter and jelly sandwiches." The man looked up quite surprised and responded, "I'm not married."*

We're all packing our own lunches, and it's our choice what we pack in our lunches every day.

Many people take High Performance Training to enhance their communication skills, tap their creativity, or achieve their goals. What they gain is enhanced self-esteem which makes all other things possible. An out-of-work salesman applied for a job with my company. After he heard what he would be selling he said, "I can't sell this training. I need to take it!" He had been fired from his last position and his self-esteem was very low. After he took the training he opened his company and is highly successful. A little self-esteem goes a long way!

A woman who went through the training was interested in only the networking possibilities. Her husband had left her after twenty-two years, devastating her. She completed the training, got a job with one of our graduates and remarried shortly thereafter. Self-esteem can help in any situation.

We all gather our self-esteem from several areas of our lives. Each of us has areas that are more important to us than others. Some of us take our self-esteem from our work—how we feel about our position, promotions, responsibility, supervisors, co-workers, as well as

49

our ability to support our family. Another area where we gather self-esteem is from our social life. Our social relationships with other individuals, neighbors, club members, sports teams, and friends provide self-esteem. Others base self-esteem on personal relationships with spouse, children, parents, grandparents and other close ties. Wherever you gather your self-esteem, it's important to remember that negative experiences in any of these areas tend to lower your self-esteem. Positive experiences raise your self-esteem. There isn't one single occurrence of any event that will determine your level of self-esteem. Self-esteem develops over time, constantly changing based on your experiences.

No matter what your level of self-esteem is now, you can take steps to enhance and improve it. I have used several techniques to build my self-esteem which I've learned from others. I'll share these with you. Use the techniques that work best for you. Modify them to fit your needs.

REFRAME NEGATIVES INTO POSITIVES

Reframe and nurture your belief system. Low self-esteem and a negative self-image come from your thoughts. You are what you think about all day long. Start by keeping a Judgment Journal. Use a notebook or piece of paper. Every day for one week pay attention to the negative judgments you make about yourself or others.

You'll be amazed at the number of negative judgments you make in one week's time! These judgments might include such things as: "I can't pay my bills," "I hate exercising," "That was stupid," "I wish I could get a promotion," "I'll never find a wife," "I can't speak to groups; I always go blank." Judgments you might make of others include "Why doesn't he get a job?" "He's greedy," "She's too aggressive," "They're boring," "Nice hairdo," "He's incompetent," "She's fat." We state negative judgments to ourselves all day long and never realize it.

I tell people in our training course that no matter what else they walk away with, at least they will have achieved a new level of awareness. Awareness about themselves and their lives. Awareness of how they treat themselves and others.

After you keep the Judgment Journal for a week, keep a Victory Log for a week. Write down every success you have during the day. Not just big successes like getting a new job or big raise. I mean getting your son to pick up his room, making five cold calls, paying someone a compliment, finishing everything on your TO DO list, or even cleaning that messy closet. Keep track of your daily victories. It's amazing how wonderful you feel after you see how much you accomplish in just one day, let alone a week.

Now, sit down and look at the patterns in your judgments. You'll find that you are making the same types of statements frequently. Reframe them to be positive. For instance, if you say to yourself, "That woman is fat," reframe that to say, "That woman deserves to be thinner." If you say to yourself, "I am disorganized," reframe that and say, "I am becoming more organized every day." We'll take this a step further in the next exercise.

REPROGRAMMING YOUR SUBCONSCIOUS MIND

Now feed the reframed statements into your subconscious mind. Keep in mind that in our conscious mind we make decisions; in our subconscious mind we find the answers. The conscious mind takes care of the following processes: reason, logic, form, judgment, calculation, conscience, and moral sense. The subconscious mind takes care of intuition, emotion, certitude, inspiration, suggestion, deduction, imagination, and memory.

When reprogramming the subconscious mind for success, it is important to remember three universal laws about the subconscious mind.

First: The conscious mind is the rational chooser and the subconscious mind is the irrational prover. Whatever the conscious mind tells the subconscious mind, the subconscious mind will prove it. It's been said, *"If you will make the decision, your subconscious will make the provision."*

Second: The subconscious mind will believe anything you tell it. Remember when reprogramming the subconscious mind for success, the statements you make must be useful, but they need not be accurate.

Third: Reinforce only the positive. Instead of saying, "I want to quit smoking," which reinforces the fact that you are a smoker, simply say, "I am a non-smoker and I enjoy breathing fresh air."

Make yourself a complete list of the negative statements you say to yourself and reframe them to be positive and in the present tense. You can change your belief system by reframing and stating, or feeding, these new statements back into your subconscious mind. A good time to do this is just as you go to sleep at night, when you are relaxed and have no distractions. Use the following page to write out your negative statements and then to reframe them into positive, present tense statements.

List limiting statements about yourself that you either now or at one time have believed. Rewrite each of these statements as a positive affirmation. Make sure the reframed statement is in the positive and present tense. You can also put down statements that state, "I am becoming," or "I deserve to be," for example.

SUBCONSCIOUS PROGRAM	SUBCONSCIOUS RE-PROGRAM
I am broke	I am prosperous
I am clumsy	I am graceful
I am sick	I am healthy
I am disorganized	I am becoming organized
I am lazy	I deserve to be energetic

1. _____   _____

2. _____   _____

3. _____   _____

4. _____   _____

5. _____   _____

6. _____   _____

7. _____   _____

8. _____   _____

9. _____   _____

10. _____   _____

11. _____   _____

12. _____   _____

13. _____   _____

14. _____   _____

15. _____   _____

16. _____   _____

17. _____   _____

18. _____   _____

19. _____   _____

20. _____   _____

Your subconscious programming will set the tone for the rest of your life. It's your choice: whether you want your life to be rich and full, or empty and negative. Here's a story about a King that shows how simple it is to change your programming positively:

> A long time ago, there was a young King who was deformed. He had a severe hunchback, and his appearance was offensive to many people in his kingdom. He commissioned a famous sculptor to sculpt his figure. When the sculptor arrived the King told him he wanted the sculpture to be of him standing up straight and looking handsome and proud. The sculptor was hesitant to change his model's appearance, but he finally agreed. Several years later the sculptor was being honored for another piece of his work and he ran into a man who worked for that young King. The man stated that it was a handsome piece he had done of the King and the sculptor replied, "Well yes, but it's too bad that he is really so hunched over and deformed." The man looked surprised and said, "What are you talking about? I've worked for the King for several years and he is quite handsome and normal."
>
> Later the sculptor found out that the King had used the sculpture of himself to change his thinking and appearance. Everyday he went to the garden and looked at the sculpture of himself looking handsome and normal. Over time that's what he became.

You can change your old programming and work miracles for

yourself. Reframing and reprogramming your subconscious mind allows you to take control of your belief system and your life.

BUILDING "I AM" STATEMENTS

Another excellent technique to use for building self-esteem is to create a list of positive statements about yourself. "I am confident," "I am strong," "I am smart," "I am loving." After you compile the list, read it into a tape recorder. If you have a difficult time thinking of traits you want or have, look in the appendix at the list I've supplied. This will create a personal "I am" tape that you can play first thing in the morning, in your car, or any time you need a boost. If you can't think of enough positive attributes that you have, or you would like to have, there is a long list in the back of this book from which to choose. If you want to state an attribute that you feel you don't have then simply say, "I deserve to be confident," or "I am becoming more confident every day." Be creative with your "I am" tape by putting your favorite music or sounds behind your voice. This is my favorite self-esteem booster. Listening to "I am" statements in your own voice will help you to accept the information approximately eighty-seven percent faster!

VARIATIONS

Another technique you can use with that same list of "I am's" is to stand in front of a mirror and make the statements while watching yourself. It's very powerful to look yourself right in the eye and say, "I am dynamic."

A variation of this technique is to sing your favorite song, one that makes you feel confident or motivated, while facing yourself in the mirror. Use emotion and inflection to make it even more powerful.

Another variation is to remember positive things others have told you—a mentor, teacher, or a close friend for whom you have great respect. What would they say to you now? What did they say to you in the past? It is powerful to imagine, or remember, what someone you respect has said or would say to you.

ANCHORING HIGH PERFORMANCE STATES

The next technique I'd like to share with you comes from neurolinguistic programming. NLP is a dynamic technology that is excellent for creating personal change. NLP is basically your communication with yourself and with others. It has reached a level of acceptance through-out the professional world, helping individuals overcome fear and anx-iety and to communicate more effectively. I suggest several techniques from NLP throughout this system. The technique that I'll share first is anchoring.

Close your eyes and remember a time when you did something extremely well. A time when you felt totally confident and in charge. Recall the feelings you had at that time. The feelings of self-confidence and pride. See yourself in the scene with your friends smiling and sharing your pride. Hear them congratulate you and tell you what a good job you've done. Now, in your mind's eye, make the picture big-ger and brighter, with bold colors. Intensify the feelings. Place your middle finger and thumb of your left hand together and hold it while you intensify the picture, feelings and sounds. When you have the pic-ture as bright as you can make it, and the feelings as intense as pos-sible you've reached what is called a state of excellence, or a High Performance State. Hold on to this scene as long as you can. The anchor will be easier to reinstate when the feelings are as intense as possible.

What we have done is to create an anchor. Every time you want to bring back these wonderful feelings, building your self-esteem, simply place your finger and thumb together. This action will bring back those feelings of excellence that you have anchored.

We have anchors created for us all the time. Have you ever gotten goose bumps when you hear "The Star Spangled Banner" or "America the Beautiful"? These are anchors. Advertisers create anchors for us all the time. Remember the commercials for greeting cards that tug at your heartstrings? Or the coffee advertisement with the son coming home from the army and surprising his family? These are touching and create powerful anchors for us with the advertiser's product. What we want to do is to create positive anchors for ourselves by imprinting positive pictures, feelings and sounds, that we can recall whenever we need them. Anchors can become diluted over time, so it's important to go through this exercise occasionally to rebuild or rein-state your anchor.

CHANGING NEGATIVE EXPERIENCES

We all have negative experiences we live with every day. They might stem from criticisms, embarrassing moments, or mistakes you've made. Whatever the negative situation is, you can put it behind you or you can reimprint it. Our experiences are imprinted in our memory like etchings on a piece of glass or a mirror. They are always there, and they can be extremely vivid. The interesting thing about these negative experiences is that we have a tendency to relive them any time something similar arises. What we want to do as High Performers is to reimprint these experiences. For our purposes we won't go through changing the experience and making it positive; we'll simply put it behind us.

I had an experience when I was in the sixth grade which I have carried with me and relived as if it had just happened. This experience held me back until I learned this technique. I was in the sixth grade and was so excited when I was the only sixth grader invited to an eighth grade party. I got all dressed up and my dad was going to drive me to the party since we lived out in the country and it was several miles away. The house where the party was to be held was back a long lane. My dad dropped me off and left. I sheepishly walked up to the door and rang the bell. A woman came to the door and asked what I wanted. I looked around and could see that there was not going to be a party in this house. I told her I was there for Jan's party and she said, "Didn't anyone call you? The party was cancelled because Jan has the measles." At that moment I felt as if I was two inches tall. No one had bothered to call the lowly sixth grader. I felt so embarrassed and stupid I thought I would die right on the spot. The lady gave me a ride home so the agony lasted for nearly one hour.

For years after that experience, any time I was criticized or embarrassed or made a mistake I relived that experience as if it was just happening. I could see myself in the scene, in vivid color. I could feel the pressure of my blood rising to my face. So of course, I would back off or cry or run away. This is a real good picture of a strong professional! Then I learned how to put this experience behind me, literally. Here's how it goes:

Sit down in a quiet place for this exercise, some place where you will not be interrupted. Now, remember a time when you had a negative experience. Maybe it was an embarrassing situation or the day your boss fired you.

Whatever the situation, put yourself directly in the scene. Get a clear picture in your mind. Do you see the picture in color or black and white? Is it clear or fuzzy? Can you feel the feelings you felt? Now, make the picture black and white. Turn down the volume and make the picture smaller. Make the picture as small as a postage stamp. Next, in your mind, take the tiny picture and move it over your shoulder and put it behind you and keep moving it back further and further until you can no longer see it. How does it seem now? Can you feel the feelings? Does it seem recent? Probably not. Go through this exercise as many times as necessary to lessen the impact of the negative situation. As new situations arise you can put them behind you using this technique.

I believe this technique has completely changed my life. Now when something negative happens to me, I don't play back that old hurt. I simply put it behind me and move forward, a little wiser and a lot happier.

STRATEGY FOR HANDLING CRITICISM

Criticism is something you deal with nearly every day. You might receive criticism from your boss, a co-worker, your spouse, your child, your neighbor or even your best friend. Being able to handle this criticism effectively is helpful in attaining success. Every time you receive criticism it chips away at your self-esteem and eventually erodes it away. Here's a tool to help you learn to handle criticism effectively either on the job or at home.

1. When someone begins to criticize you, **disassociate from the scene.** In your mind, watch yourself being criticized by this other person. Many people have a tendency to associate with the pain of criticism and this makes it much more difficult to handle.

2. Once you've disassociated from the action of criticism, **watch the scene and listen to the criticism.** This is happening quickly, so listen carefully.

3. **Ask yourself questions** like, "What is the criticism? Is it something that I did or forgot to do? Was it I or someone else who did it? Is this person typically critical of me?"

4. **Evaluate** the answers to the questions. "Did I do it or was it my fault?"

5. **Reassociate with the scene.** Come back to being in the scene.

6. Respond to the criticism **rationally and logically.**

Going through these steps will help you eliminate the negative feelings associated with criticism. You can keep from taking it personally. When I discuss gender-blending you will find that men have a tendency to do this strategy naturally. Women, on the other hand, have a tendency to associate fully with the pain, and therefore take criticism as personal attacks. Try this technique and practice it before you get caught in another critical situation.

IMAGERY

Imagery is simply creating pictures in your mind. You can use these pictures to your benefit. They can build your self-esteem, protect you from criticism or verbal attacks, or provide you with a stress-free environment. Let's say you want to build your self-esteem by using imagery. Go to a quiet place where you will not be interrupted. Close your eyes and relax. Imagine that you are completely coated in gold. This gold coating is extremely valuable. You can then add "I am" statements to your image and say, "I am worthwhile and important."

Maybe you want to use imagery to eliminate stress from your work. While you are in your quiet place, imagine you are in the shower and the water is washing all the stressors down the drain. Or, imagine you are under a waterfall and the water is washing all the stress away from you.

The best part of imagery is that it is completely yours. You can design it to fit your particular situation and needs. You can use it anywhere, and anytime. Be creative with your imagery. Add symbolism to strengthen it and make it your own. If you have a hard time seeing pictures in your mind, just feel the sensations, or listen to the sounds and pictures will eventually come to your mind.

SHARING COMPLIMENTS

Another way to build your self-esteem is to share compliments with others. We spend much of our time looking for what others have done wrong, when we should be looking for what they have done right. Share compliments with the people around you. Make sure you're sincere. Let me share a story with you about the word "sincere."

> In Italy, many years ago, there was a very fine line of pottery statues created. The statues were extremely beautiful and people loved owning them. Well, as things go, some of the statues got broken. The owners were upset and finally someone developed a fine wax to mend the broken statues. This was such a fine wax that once a statue was repaired, no one could tell it was ever broken. Only experts could tell the mended statues from the unbroken pieces. This caused the

*price of the unbroken statues to sky rocket, because
they were sin cerre' (without wax).*

Make sure when you share a compliment that it is "sin cerré," or
"without wax."

ACCEPTING COMPLIMENTS

The next thing is to simply accept compliments. What do you typically say when someone gives you a compliment? "Oh, this old thing?"
You immediately minimize, or negate the complimenter and the compliment. You not only put yourself down by doing this, you also put the
other person down by making them feel as if they don't know what
they're talking about.

When I started writing articles for a small newspaper, a friend told
me that they were very good. What did I say? "Oh, that was nothing."
Of course it was. I worked really hard on those articles. When you
receive a compliment—really receive it! All you have to say is "THANK
YOU!"

Complimenting is a lost art. Sharing a compliment can make you
and others feel great. I encourage everyone in my training classes to
share compliments. We even practice giving and receiving compliments. Here are some basic points you should remember for sharing
effective compliments:

- **Be sincere when you are complimenting.** Make sure
  the person knows you are being honest and want
  nothing in return.

- **Smile when you share compliments.** Smiling shows
  that you are open and friendly, and carries a gentle
  warmth.

- **Make eye contact with the person.** This helps build
  your credibility and sincerity.

- **Touch the person you're complimenting.** People like
  to be touched, as long as it's appropriate touching.
  Even a subtle touch on the hand lets the person feel
  your sincerity.

- **Compliment the person, not their clothes.** Instead
  of saying, "I really like that shirt," say, "You look ter-
  rific in that shirt." This adds a more personal touch.

- **Don't compliment continuously.** When you over

compliment, the compliments become diluted, seeming insincere. Make sure you compliment, but don't overdo it.

- **Compliment a person in front of others.** When you publicly compliment, it makes the compliment even better.

- **Don't make complimenting a part of your weekly schedule.** Complimenting needs to be spontaneous in order to be effective. When you schedule compliments, they seem contrived and insincere.

- **Share the compliments you receive with others.** When you are complimented for doing a good job and you know others helped you—share the glory.

- **When someone compliments you, all you need to say is "Thank you."**

- **Compliment your staff, your peers, your spouse, your kids.** Complimenting isn't just for work, it's for everyone in your life.

- **Think of your compliments as verbal hugs.**

We all have the ability to make others feel good. This wonderful feeling comes back to you many times over. I'd like to conclude with a final story:

> Willie Davis, the all-time great running back, was in Los Angeles when he got the word that his former coach, Vince Lombardi, was near death in Washington, D. C. Willie jumped on a red-eye flight to D. C. He knew he wouldn't get to spend much time with Lombardi. In fact when he arrived he was allowed only two minutes with his former coach. Lombardi had slipped into a coma. Davis left the hospital returning to Los Angeles. At the airport a reporter asked Davis why he would fly all that way just to look at a man who didn't even realize he was there? Davis looked at the reporter and said, "I had to. That man made me feel like SOMEBODY!"

I challenge you to make someone feel like SOMEBODY.

ACTION PAGE

The great aim of education is not knowledge, but ACTION.
-Herbert Spencer

ACTION STEPS
To High Performance

The major benefit I gained from this chapter was:

_____

_____

_____

_____

Based on this benefit, my High Performance Action Plan is:

_____

_____

_____

_____

Why is this action plan important to me?

_____

_____

_____

_____

Chapter 5

Communication: The Ultimate Advantage

Communication is a process of
establishing common understanding.
Paul R. Trimm

We have learned that eighty-seven per cent of our success is based on our ability to communicate effectively. With this in mind, it's easy to understand why communication is the ultimate advantage. Research shows that only seven percent of our communication is verbal. The other ninety-three per cent is non-verbal—everything we say without uttering a word. Because our non-verbal communication is so significant, as High Performers we focus on the ninety-three percent. Communication comes from the Latin word meaning to make common. As a High Performer you should focus on the other person to develop commonality. This way you can achieve true understanding and become more effective communicators.

Communication, because it is so much a part of our make up, can become difficult in any environment. In a professional setting it's crucial. Your communication on the job will set the stage for your entire career. Learning to communicate effectively is absolutely necessary. To help you understand the communication process, experts have designed a universal model which I have interpreted as follows.

Encoding ——▶**Transmitting** ——▶**Receiving** ——▶**Decoding**
(Sender)   **(Receiver)**

You transmit your message via a medium. The receiver then interprets the message, or attaches meaning to it. As your message is transmitted, it goes through something called a barrier or filter. This barrier distorts your original meaning of the message. By the time it gets to the receiver, a new meaning has been attached to your message. To make sure the receiver gets the message you intended, it's necessary to identify and understand these potential communication filters or barriers:

1. Environment

2. Listening skills

3. Communication styles

4. Gender of the sender and receiver

Understanding these potential filters, or barriers, to effective communication is vital. I'll cover some specific items dealing with each filter.

ENVIRONMENT

When you communicate you must be aware of your environment. The environment in which your communication takes place can affect the communication itself. Many items in the environment can be distractors, for instance—

On the job

    Noise from faxes, printers, phones, talking

    Anxiety, fear, joy

    Visual surroundings

At home

    Television

    Children playing/talking

    Cars, toys

Consider the following scenarios:

Scene 1

You're running late and you've just gotten to work. Three people are lined up at your office door with questions needing immediate answers. Your phone is ringing. Your secretary's phone is ringing. The fax is running. Two copiers are running large jobs. A maintenance worker is pounding as he hangs your new marker board. Your boss barges into your office to give you some important information about your presentation due in an hour. Your boss's message to you is, "Make sure you present the numbers from the latest marketing report."

Scene 2

You just got home from work. The kids are fighting. The television is playing loudly. Someone is knocking on the front door. The neighbor is mowing his yard. Your husband is running the blender. The phone rings. As you answer it you hear a loud crash from the basement. Then you hear a voice at the other end of the phone asking what long distance carrier you use.

In either of these scenarios, communication is being filtered in a variety of ways. This isn't unusual. When your message to another person is important, make sure you are in the proper environment to ensure the communication is successful. If your environment can't be changed that moment, stop and focus on the person. Ask him if he understands. Ask him to repeat the message back to you.

It is always the responsibility of the sender to make sure the communication is understood as it was intended.

LISTENING SKILLS

Another thing to strive for in your communication as a High Performer is effective listening skills. Listening, psychologists have found, is the part of communication most often used during an average day. Most of us spend 42 percent of our time each day listening, 32 percent talking, 15 percent reading, and 11 percent writing. From this we conclude that we need to become experts at listening. Yet, statistics tell us that we miss 85 percent of what we hear.

What is involved in listening well? First, you must hear what the other person is saying. Second, you must understand what is being said. Third, you must remember what has been said. Here are some tips to help you become a better listener.

1. Encourage dialogue with eye contact and expression.

This is simply expressing interest. You can show this interest in a variety of ways.

Maintaining eye contact is a very important way. A nod of your head or a brief yes, or good point, in a one-on-one situation is a good idea. In a group, lean forward to show interest.

2. Listen intently, concentrating on the individual and what is being said.

Try not to evaluate what the person is saying. Instead, concentrate on what is being said. Listen for the main point without evaluating or judging. Don't worry about what you are going to say next...you'll get your turn.

3. Summarize and seek clarification periodically.

The average speaker usually talks at a rate of 250 words per minute. The average listener, however, can listen at a rate of 400 to 450 words per minute. This difference allows the listener's mind to wander. To avoid this, try asking questions or restating the speaker's key points, such as "So what I hear you saying is—" This is called paraphrasing.

Active listening is very important to the communication process. Listening to understand and retain is what makes you a High Performance communicator.

COMMUNICATION STYLES

I mentioned earlier that the technology of neurolinguistic programming provides us with a model for powerful communication. NLP teaches that every individual communicates in one of three styles or modalities. Understanding this very important information about the way we are wired will help you communicate more effectively. As I stated earlier, there are three basic communication styles or modalities: visual, auditory and kinesthetic. We each have some traits of all these styles, but we are stronger, or more dominant, in one. The way we present information is also the way we prefer to receive information. Read this information until you feel comfortable with it.

Our communication style is how we actually represent ourselves to the rest of the world. When you communicate with others, you will typically use your dominant style to get your point across. To become high performance communicators, it's necessary to communicate in the other person's style. In the new business environment, and in today's relationships, it is critical to gain the understanding of these styles. To become chameleons in communicating. When you communicate in the listener's style, you develop rapport. Rapport allows effective communication to occur. Communication flows easily and is natural. If you and the listener are communicating in different styles, you will have a mismatch. The listener will not understand the communication, and you're guaranteed to fail.

Here's a look at each of the communications styles. It will help you understand the attributes of each style so you can easily identify them. Again, keep in mind, we all have a little of each style within us. If you'd like to study this further I recommend you read *Instant Rapport*, a book by Michael Brooks.

Visuals. There are more visuals than any other style. Visuals make up sixty percent of the population. (I'm told I'm a flaming visual!) Clearly, you'll deal with visuals more frequently than the other two styles. The visual speaks rapidly. Sometimes visuals speak so rapidly they leave out words.

Visuals use words like "see," "picture," or "clear" that describe or imply seeing. As a visual myself, I use phrases like, "See what I mean?" Or "Do you have a clear picture of what I'm saying?" Visuals tend to do things quicker. They like to keep moving. Sometimes it seems as if visuals move quicker than the speed of life.

The visual person will walk into a room and straighten pictures on the wall. Visuals tend to put importance on the way things look. When I buy clothes, I buy first because of the way something looks. If it looks good to me, then I might try it on to see if it feels all right. I tend to wear brighter color clothing. I like things to be neat and tidy. I will pick lint or stray hairs from your lapel or shoulder. I may have stacks on my desk, but they are neat stacks. As a visual I'm not fond of casual touching.

Visuals tend to be a little more dramatic in communication. They use expressive language and lots of gestures, showing much enthusiasm. When they gesture, they tend to gesture in an upward motion. Many times you can watch closely and see that when they are accessing pictures in their minds, they tend to stop breathing, or breathe shallowly. If you're a visual, you might point to your eyes when you're explaining or asking questions. You might rub your eyes or neck if you don't understand something.

In learning, the visual must see to understand. It is important for you to give them a graph or show them in writing so they will understand. When you show appreciation to a visual, give them something so they can see that you mean what you're saying.

Auditories. This group of communicators make up less than twenty percent of the population. They have a tendency to speak in a level tonality, but not a monotone. They are the true listeners of the world. Sounds can please the auditory or drive them crazy. They are in tune with their environment. They use words like "sound," "hear," or "click." They tend to be graceful individuals who like harmony. Auditories like variety in their speech tones, and the tones of others.

In general auditories are the most difficult style with whom to communicate. You must be a good orator to please the auditory. If they don't hear what you're saying, they tend to give you a blank look or no feedback at all. This can be very frustrating.

The auditory will hold her ears if she doesn't like a sound. She will gesture less and at shoulder or chest height. Auditories are also neat individuals. When they move, they seem to flow gracefully. They will relate happenings, or timeframes, to music or sound. They tend to talk internally before they see pictures in their minds.

Kinesthetics. OHHH the kinesthetics! The person who is in touch with his feelings. The kinesthetic is a person who speaks very, very slowly—and drives the visual crazy. The kinesthetic will use words in conversation like "feel," "grasp," or "sense." They are the hands-on people who love sports and doing. They tend to have a lower pitch to their voice. You might catch a kinesthetic with his head in his hands or rubbing his face. They have turned pausing into a fine art.

Kinesthetics tend to gesture slower and lower. They tend to gesture downward as they are getting into their feelings. They will buy clothing based on the way it feels. If it feels good, they will keep it for fifty years! They have a tendency to wear more earth tones and casual styles. The comfortable style and look of the typical psychologist is the look of the kinesthetic.

My husband Tom is highly kinesthetic. Before we were aware of these styles we didn't communicate well. Remember, I am a visual. I would talk rapidly and Tom's eyes would glaze over. I thought he was stupid! Of course he isn't stupid. He simply processes at a slower rate of speed than I do.

Tom always thought that if he was responsible and dependable, I would feel he loves me. Boy, was he wrong! As a visual, I need to be taken places, or bought flowers, to know that he loves me.

You can see how mismatches occur. I worked with a woman who

owned a print shop. She was a visual. She hired a man to do the printing. He started work two hours earlier each day then she did. In her visual manner, she created a beautiful form on which she wrote in detail his daily assignments. However, she noticed that every day the printer would come to her asking her what he was to do for the day. She'd become frustrated and ask, "Can't you read? Just look at this form!" The printer would reply, "Just tell me what you want me to do. I don't understand what you're saying." Obviously the printer was an auditory and needed to hear the instructions. I recommended she throw out the form and simply record the instructions into a tape recorder. Now the printer listens to the recording each day, and their communications go smoothly.

EYE MOVEMENTS

The eyes are the window to the soul. Eyes can identify what style of communicator you are. Each of the three communication styles has wired-in eye movements. This diagram demonstrates the eye movements of each style. The following list will let you know what to expect from each style.

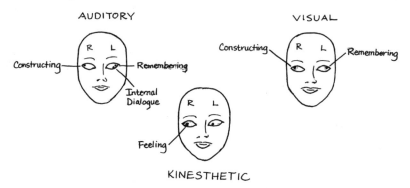

Eye Accessing Cues

Visual

Eyes up to right	remembering
Eyes up to left	constructing

Auditory

Level and right	constructing
Down and left	self talk
Level and left	remembering

Kinesthetic

Down and right	feelings

EXERCISE

Use this diagram to determine the dominant style of your friend or co-worker. Ask your partner questions that will require her to remember things and to construct things. Examples are: Tell me about your first car. What was it like to ride your first bike? Imagine your mother with green hair...what do you think? You're sitting in a red Lamborgini, imagine it's yours ánd tell me what you think. As your partner answers the questions, watch her eye movements. Many people will begin in an upward movement of the eyes and then settle into their dominant style. Make small marks to show where her eyes went as she responded. Also, listen to the types of words she uses, especially the verbs. The words on the next page give you an example of the different styles. If you get a conflict between the eye movements and the words she uses...go with the words. The words will be much more accurate.

Left-handed people will do the exact opposite. Make sure you identify her hand dominance before you begin.

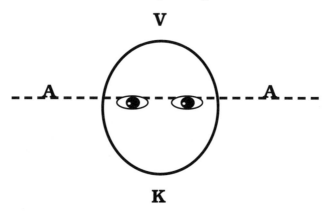

VAK SENSORY SYSTEMS

Sensory systems are used by people to think about, and communicate their experience. These sensory systems are expressed in the words we use, especially the verbs and adjectives.

VISUAL	AUDITORY	KINESTHETIC
see	hear	feel
look	listen	touch
appear	tell	catch on
imagine	ask	contact

| perspective | sounds | rub |
| reveal | in tune | push |

Words that imply visualization	Words that imply sounds	Words that imply feelings & sensations
color	harmony	happy
sparkle	silence	curious
clear	clicks	warm

When you are aware of the other person's style you can speak to him in his style rather than your own. My clients tell me that sometimes this is difficult. They say it's difficult to carry on a conversation and pay attention to what words the other person is using. I always tell them, Exactly! That's what good communication is all about and it isn't easy! The more you concentrate on the other person, the better the communication will be. Practice this and you'll see what I mean. Soon it will become second nature to you. I can now spot a visual within thirty seconds! You'll soon be able to use this tool like a pro.

VAK SELF-TEST

Answer the following questions to determine your dominant style. Use your first response and answer honestly to get the best results. After you have completed the test, total the A's, B's and C's and write the number in the space provided. The answer is provided at the end of the test.

1. Your dream house has the following—
     _____ A) etched windows, built-in appliances, and colorful walls.
     _____ B) Large, open rooms, soft carpet.
     _____ C) built-in stereo system and wind chimes on the porch.

2. When you buy a new car you always—
     _____ A) look at the color and style first.
     _____ B) sit in the car to feel its roominess.
     _____ C) play the radio and listen to the engine.

3. When you get dressed for work you usually—

_____✓ A) wear bright colors.

_____ B) put on the most comfortable suit.

_____৲ C) make sure you are neat and tidy.

4. When getting feedback in a conversation, you often ask—

_____ A) do you see what I'm saying?

_____৲ B) do you understand the essence of the informa-
tion?

_____✓ C) do you hear what I'm saying?

5. When you meet someone new, you notice his—

_____✓ A) clothes, hair, and shoes.

_____ B) confidence, poise, and ability to make you feel
comfortable.

_____ C) voice and tonality.

6. You walk into a room and the first thing you want to do is—

_____✓ A) straighten a crooked picture on the wall.

_____ B) sit down in a comfortable chair.

_____৲ C) listen for a welcoming sound.

TOTALS   A's _4_   B's _____   C's _____

If you answered mostly A's, you are probably visual, B's kinesthetic, and C's auditory. Use this in conjunction with the eye movements and the word identification to be accurate.

GENDER STYLES IN COMMUNICATION AND LEADERSHIP

	MEN Left Brain	WOMEN Right Brain	
High Power			New Paradigm

COMMUNICATION	LEADERSHIP
12,000 words/day	Support
Internal problem solving	Vision
Large gestures	Solution orientation
Disassociate pain	People
Less smiling	Whole picture
High touch	Intuitive
Low pitch	Involvement
Few facial expressions	Cooperate

LEADERSHIP	COMMUNICATION
Direct	25,000 words/day
Goals	External problem solving
Problem orientation	Small gestures
Things	Associate pain
Bottom line	More smiling
Logical	Low touch
Independence	High pitch
Negotiate	More facial expressions

Gender-blending: mixing of gender strengths
to obtain a desired combination of qualities.

Low
Power

Old
Paradigm

Recently there's been much talk about gender differences. Indeed there are differences and because of those differences, some of them must be blended in order to achieve success in the 90's. Here is a diagram of gender leadership and communication styles.

As you can see from this diagram, men and women in business have some distinct challenges facing them when it comes to communication and leadership. These differences act as filters, or barriers, to effective communication. In business it is becoming increasingly important for companies to develop team work and an environment of empowerment. When gender-blending occurs, both men and women will be more successful with teams and customers in the new service economy. The blending of communication styles will help women develop power leading to greater respect, credibility and status. It will assist men in developing the skills necessary to build rapport, nurture team members, and build strong leadership traits which are important in the new business network.

This gender-blending will also help men and women in relationships. When they learn to communicate in a rapport building style, both sexes will be happier.

COMMUNICATION REALITY

When you get right down to it, communication is at best quite difficult. For instance, consider this communication:

*I know you believe you understand what you think I
said, but I am not sure you realize that what you
heard is not what I meant!*

This exercise in written communication will help you practice your communication skills. Here is an exercise that will help you be more perceptive to the written word.

Count the number of F's in the following paragraph:

FINISHED FILES ARE THE
RESULT OF YEARS OF
SCIENTIFIC STUDY COMBINED
WITH THE EXPERIENCE
OF MANY YEARS,
(Answer located in Appendix A)

If you didn't get the right answer the first time, reread the statement slowly, looking at each word carefully. In written communication as well as verbal, we tend to skip words. We tend to hear or see what we want.

As a High Performer you should focus clearly on the communication process each and every time you send a message. Communication and understanding must become a priority in order for you to do it successfully. Consider what research tells us about retention of data.

Retention of Data:	3 hours later	3 days later
Oral Communication	25%	10%
Visual Communication	72%	20%
Oral and Visual Communication	85%	65%

You can see the significant jump in retention when you use both oral and visual communication. Remember to use many styles of communication, and to be as vivid as possible.

NON-VERBAL COMMUNICATION

Paul R. Trimm, in his book on managerial communication, defined six areas of non-verbal communication. It's important to understand all six to attain the high performance edge.

Ninety-three percent of our communication is non-verbal. Only seven percent is verbal; the words we say. Understanding non-verbal communication is extremely important to us. There are so many things that we say without ever uttering a word. People watch us and our non-verbal communication contradicts the words we say. Or it overpowers what we say. People will make judgments about you based on your appearance or the movements that you make. They might judge your confidence, intelligence, social status, integrity, morals, or your sexual proclivity. (This is why a low-cut blouse or a tight sweater is inappropriate for a job interview). When you are being judged, you want to put your best foot forward.

Here are the six areas of non-verbal communication—

Classifications-

> **1. Body motion or kinesic. Gestures, facial expressions, body movements.**
>
> **2. Paralanguage. Voice qualities, laughing, yawning.**
>
> **3. Proxemics. Physical space.**

4. Olfaction. Smell.

5. Skin sensitivity. Stroking, hitting, hand shaking.

6. Artifacts. Clothes, eyeglasses, jewelry.

Following are some tips for each of these areas to help you gain power in your communication style. Because non-verbal communication is so powerful, it's important to use as many of these tips as possible. You'll speak with power and authority in any situation.

Body motion. The way you move your body will tell people you are confident, intelligent and savvy. Or it will say you are weak, lack confidence and are unimportant. What does it say about you if you walk into a room hunched over, dragging your feet, with your shoulders drooping and head hung down? You don't appear to have much confidence; you're not intelligent; and you're lazy. Just on entering a room! Change that scene and walk into the room with your head held high, shoulders up and back, brisk pace and large steps. This time you'll appear confident, intelligent and with a sense of urgency.

As a High Performer you need to practice your body movements. If you've spent most of your life walking in a low power style, it will take some time to change those habits. Have a friend critique the way you enter a room. Or watch yourself in a full-length mirror. When you think about body movements being important, certain people might come to mind. Perhaps Jackie Kennedy Onassis, with her elegance and grace, or Bill Clinton with his purposeful motions emphasizing points. Other confident walkers include Alec Baldwin, Tom Hanks and Sharon Stone.

Paralanguage. Your voice quality is formed when you are very young. We imitate the people we are around the most, typically our parents. If you don't like the sound of your voice, you CAN change it. Voice quality is critical to your success. If you have a high voice, practice lowering it by humming. Go as low as you can without losing quality and then begin talking. Remember the VAK? If you speak fast you're likely a visual. You won't be as effective when in a conversation with a kinesthetic. Slow down to be effective with a kinesthetic. Pay attention to the people you're speaking with. You'll make a big impact on their level of understanding. Power talking comes with a low, slow tonality. To show confidence and poise you may want to adopt this style, using pausing for a strong effect.

Proxemics. The amount of physical space you take up indicates whether you have confidence or not. According to Michael Korda in his book, *Power*, the more space you take, the more power you gain. Notice the front of Lee Iacoca's book. He's sitting in a chair, leaned back with his hands behind his head—taking up a lot of space. This gives him the appearance of confidence and power. Whoever designed the cover of his book put him in a power position! Have you ever had a person get really close to you? Does it make you feel really uncomfortable? It is so uncomfortable, we can't tolerate it. Americans are comfortable with more distance, about twelve to eighteen inches, say experts. I find that most Americans prefer an arm's length. To witness this, stand in the fast lane at the grocery store, the lane with the twelve items or less, and turn around. The people behind you will move back almost instantly. Proxemics is very important. We have to remember when we're talking with a client that proxemics are important. Make sure you give the other person her space.

Here's where some gender-blending comes in. Many women have a tendency to take up as little space as possible. Men, on the other hand, usually take up as much space as they can. My suggestion to women is, when you sit down in a meeting, put one arm over the chair next to you. Or sit up straight with both of your arms on the chair arms. Don't slump, folding your arms and legs as if you are trying to disappear. My suggestion for men is to avoid pushing this space thing too far. It can be intimidating. When you're in a conversation with a lower power skilled person, you don't want to alienate them.

When I worked at Honeywell, the managers were given their office space based on their level in the organization. More space equaled importance. Managers were constantly asking the maintenance crew to measure their offices! For those of us who didn't have an office, we jockeyed for the cubicle with the window, because the window gave the illusion of more space. Further, the corner offices with windows are the ultimate in power and prestige.

Olfaction. This is our sense of smell. It's very closely linked to our emotions and memories. That's why aroma therapy is becoming quite popular these days. People are using aromas to bring back memories and to evoke emotions. For instance, researchers have found that baby powder is a very strong emotional pull for baby boomers.

Aroma therapy is being used in a lot of ways. The Japanese are piping smells into businesses to create different reactions. Lavender is piped into nursing homes to calm people down. Citrusy smells are piped into auto manufacturers production areas to keep people alert. It wakes people up helping them to be more productive. This is especially important on second and third shifts because people have a natural tendency to become drowsy. By keeping workers more alert it significantly lowers accident rates.

The sense of smell is powerful. I recommend in a professional setting you consider unscented products. You never know who you're offending. You can upset or anger someone just by a scent that you are wearing. You may visit a client that you have a good rapport with wearing White Shoulders Cologne, your favorite. But your client's

Aunt Hilda wore White Shoulders and he hated Aunt Hilda! When he smells it, instantly strong emotions return. You appear to be the cause! It's important to be careful what scent we use. This is especially helpful for anyone in sales.

Tactile. Skin sensitivity is another area of non-verbal communication. Touching is powerful in business. Of course, the most powerful tactile thing that we do in business today is the handshake. It's the first thing that you say about yourself when you meet someone. Do you always receive a firm handshake? Or maybe a bone crusher? Did you ever receive one of those half handshakes that really turns you off? It says you're perceived as fragile, and they don't want to hurt you. It also says, "I don't really trust you so I'm not going to give you my full hand."

The proper handshake accepted in business today is to make sure the fleshy parts of the thumb are touching. It shouldn't be a bone crusher, just nice and firm and one pump; you don't need to stand there and pump away. If you do get a half handshake, go ahead and push your hand all the way in and let them know that you are confident and ready to communicate. For many years it was proper for a woman to offer her hand first. That's out the window in the business world. Now the proper etiquette is for the person who is of the higher status to offer his/her hand first. If you want to balance a handshake, whoever puts his hand out first should allow the other person to release first. Remember all this the next time you shake hands!

A simple tool to use when meeting someone to develop personal power is with eye contact. This comes from a study of human beings and their eye contact conducted by Ray Birdwhistll. In studying eye movements, Dr. Birdwhistll found that when two people come together, the first person who breaks eye contact just briefly, is the person with the perceived power. The person who breaks eye contact first and then returns to eye contact has the perceived power.

Artifacts. These are all the things we wear and place around us. Here are some tips on what to wear to gain personal power—

- **Navy blue is still the most powerful color. It builds trust and says you are a team player. Dark, rich colors are all good; however, black can be intimidating. Be careful when you choose to wear black.**

- **Gold jewelry is more powerful than silver jewelry.**

- **Anything derived from nature is more powerful than man made items. Metal is more powerful than plastic, leather is more powerful than vinyl, wool and cotton are more powerful than synthet-**

ics. (Because we are all trying to become political-
ly correct, it could be that some of these things
will change over time. Some already have—like
fur!)

Dress the way you want to be perceived. If you want to be taken
seriously, then you must be congruent with your verbal messages.
Trends may change, but people's perceptions don't. You can stay current with fashion without being trendy.

COMMUNICATING TO A GROUP

Public speaking is the number one fear of Americans. Three thousand Americans were asked what they fear the most. Here are the
responses: (1) speaking to a group (2) heights (3) insects and snakes
(4) financial problems (5) death. Apparently we'd prefer to die in a pit
of snakes rather than talk in front of a group!

High Performers will take steps to enhance their public speaking
ability. Here are fifteen of the best tips to help you experience less
stress and appear dynamic in front of a group.

1. **All speakers have anxiety.** Use this anxiety to your
   favor. To control your nervousness, and help your
   audience get involved in your talk right away, begin
   with animation or movement. Don't go into boring
   details explaining a situation, simply show your audience what happened. Continue to move freely as you
   speak in front of the group. This movement will
   switch-on the whole brain, releasing stress and helping you feel natural and at ease, while drawing your
   audience into your speech. (Use the Cook's Hook-Up
   or the Cross Crawl from the chapter on stress control.)

2. **Remember that your audiences are made up of
   visuals, auditories and kinesthetics.** It's your job to
   talk to all three. Use visual aids for the visuals, speak
   in different tones for the auditory and slow down a bit
   for the kinesthetics. Use all three types of verbs to hit
   all the different styles.

3. **Use intensity to gain interest, and show real sincerity to build trust with your audience**. You can do
   this by talking about something in which you believe.

4. **Tap into your emotions.** Truly great speakers can move their audiences to action by sharing something they associate with very strong feelings. If you're talking to a group about quitting smoking, facts and figures aren't enough. You have to share a personal story to demonstrate the impact it had on your life. This will harness your emotion to move your audience to action.

5. **Be brief beyond belief!**

6. **Start your talk with a bang!** Use an outrageous statistic or unusual story to grab your audience's attention.

7. **Use an idea map to lay out your talk**. (This is discussed in the chapter on creativity.)

8. **Use visual aids wisely.** Practice with them ahead of time so you're comfortable.

9. **Use humor.** Personal stories are much better than jokes. Aim your story specifically at your particular audience. Avoid offensive humor. Be conversational, and don't tell your audience you're going to tell them a joke.

10. **If you screw up, don't tell your audience**—just keep going.

11. **The old axiom, "Tell 'em what you're going to tell 'em, tell 'em, and tell 'em what you've told 'em," is still appropriate.**

12. **Never mislead your audience, because they will find out.**

13. **Dress up for your audience.** Your audience should know that you're their speaker just by looking at you when you enter the room.

14. **Don't read your talk word for word;** however, it's all right to jot down some notes on 4 x 6 index cards to refer to occasionally.

15. **End your story with a DUBACUZ.** That means, to tell the audience what you want them to do, based on what they will gain by doing it. Everyone wants to

know, "What's in it for me?" To end a talk simply say, "This is what I suggest you do, and this is what you will gain by doing it."

I have seen these fifteen tips turn ordinary people into extraordinary speakers. When you're prepared, you're confident (and you can be just a bit outrageous). Then people will look forward to hearing you speak.

PSYCHOLINGUISTICS

Think about the words that you use frequently. Unfortunately, many words have negative meanings attached to them by the listener at the unconscious level. Here are a few words you will want to avoid: "but," "why" and "try."

> **"But"**— Using the word "but" in a sentence negates everything you said before it. Substitute the word "and" for "but," strengthening your communication.

> **"Why"**—When you use the word "why," people become defensive. They think you're accusing them of something. Substitute "how," "who," "where," "when," or "which," to avoid the negative impact.

> **"Try"**—The word "try" really means fail. As High Performers we don't try, we do! Substitute the word "do" for "try," and you won't fail.

Other negative-impact words are over-generalizations like "always," "never," and "all." When you use these words the listener will immediately think of an answer to counter what you've said. For instance, if you say, "Our customers are always satisfied," your listener will start searching for a customer who wasn't satisfied. A better statement is: "We do our best to satisfy our customers. When there's a problem, it is handled promptly."

A word that creates action in people is the word "because." A study was conducted with people using a copy machine: One person approached another who was using the copier asking if he could use it. The person at the copier refused. However, the next person who approached asked if he could go ahead because he had to make some copies. The answer was, "OK." The only difference was that the second person added the word "because."

Other words to avoid are abstract words. Concrete words are better. Examples of each—

ABSTRACT	**CONCRETE**
love	desk
freedom	door
loyalty	calendar
progress	book

Abstract words are easily misinterpreted. They tend to be ambiguous. Concrete words are distinct and straight forward. It is impossible to completely avoid abstract words. Avoid them or follow them with more concrete descriptions.

When you're communicating, you must be aware of many things. The type of words you use are only a small part. The more you're aware of the communication process, the better you'll be received. High Performers always go for powerful communication skills to set themselves apart.

ACTION PAGE

The great aim of education is not knowledge, but ACTION.
-Herbert Spencer

ACTION STEPS
To High Performance

The major benefit I gained from this chapter was:

_____

_____

_____

_____

Based on this benefit, my High Performance Action Plan is:

_____

_____

_____

_____

Why is this action plan important to me?

_____

_____

_____

_____

Chapter 6

Human Relations Skills: The Human Factor

Become genuinely interested in other people.
Dale Carnegie

G etting along with people. Really being able to develop rapport with others is an essential step in the High Performance Success System. A business woman wanted to take my course because, she couldn't stand those people she worked with. In her words, they were hateful, back stabbers, and negative. Six weeks into the course, she made the comment that she couldn't believe how much those people at work had changed. Who really changed? She had. You have control over the actions of only one person, yourself.

I've spent most of my life watching and listening to people. The exciting thing I found out is everyone is different! The one constant I found is that there's a common thread running through everyone. People like people who are like them. No matter how different people are, they still want to be around people who are the way they are. Now, that is a dichotomy if I ever heard one!

MIRRORING/MATCHING

There was an old saying I learned in Sunday school as I was growing up, "Do unto others as you would have them do unto you." Today that is somewhat changed. Now it is, "Do unto others as they want to be done unto."

In all my research, there was one technology that stood out as the essence of a new understanding. I've read everything I could about it. The technology is neurolinguistic programming. I spend a lot of time on this technology because I believe it helps us achieve success more quickly and easily than anything else I have found.

Many NLP practitioners will attempt to teach you minute details of the subject. I believe that less is more. The less you know about this subject, the less confused you'll be, and the more you will take advantage of these simple techniques. I'll help you understand the basic elements of NLP that will help you as a person. The only things that will help you are the things that you will use. The only things that you will use are the things that you understand. I'll cover some basics of this dynamic technology allowing you to understand them thoroughly.

To build strong human relation skills you must understand a couple of principles of human nature: (1) People like to feel important; and (2) people like people who are like them. It's simple to cover both principles when you are working with others by using one simple technique from NLP. It's called "mirroring and matching" or "pacing." Remember a recent conversation with someone or a group of individuals. What do you recall about their body movements or stance? When you are speaking to someone and you feel comfortable and at ease, what do you notice about bodies, tonality, facial expressions? You probably notice that these things are similar. Typically, when you see people standing in a small group conversing, you will notice that if one person crosses her arms, most others will too.

People will unconsciously mirror and match each other because it is primal to all of us. We want to be like others. In interpersonal skills training this is called rapport building. In order to achieve a good interaction with another person, we must first build rapport by gaining common ground. This is true in sales, personal relationships, and casual conversations. Unfortunately, we are creatures of habit. We have a tendency to use the same body gestures continuously. When we first meet someone we may not always match him close enough to gain rapport. Or, we are stressed out and are concerned only with ourselves at the time. It is important to consciously think about and practice using the mirroring and matching technique on a daily basis.

Here's how it works. When you meet someone new and begin a conversation, make sure you match his body stance, tone of voice, and gestures. I'm not referring to mocking or mimicking. Don't make every little move that he makes or he will move out of rapport from you. Very subtly, match the way he is standing. If he is standing with his arms crossed high on his chest, then you can stand with your arms or hands crossed lower on your body. If he has his hands in his pockets, try placing only one of your hands in a pocket. Use the same tone of voice that he uses. If he speaks softly, lower your tone a bit. If he is speaking a little gruffer, then speak a little louder. Match the intensity in his voice, not the emotion.

I demonstrate this in our classes taking two volunteers out of the classroom. I explain that the volunteers will return to the room and will be asked to carry on a conversation with each other. These people have never met before. They're instructed to ask questions and get to know each other. The audience is instructed to watch for every non-verbal movement that the volunteers make which is similar. This demonstration works so well, people will almost always come up with all of the following things that were similar: head nodding, tonality, facial expressions, hand movements or placement, leaning forward or back in the chair, leg crossing or movement, and the speed at which the two speak.

It is possible to take this to many levels. Here are the areas that you can match or pace—

Body postures	**Match part or all of another person's stance**
Gestures	**Match all or part of another's body movements**
Rhythm	**Match the rhythm or flow of another's movements**
Breathing	**Match the pace or rhythm of another's breathing**
Voice	**Match the qualities of tonality, tempo, inflection, speed**
Sensory systems	**Match the communication style of another**
Language	**Match the syntax, style, and/or idioms**

As professionals, it's not necessary to match another person to this level for everyday interactions. If you want to become an NLP guru, go for it! Just know that it's the simple parts that make this technology easy to use.

Developing rapport is a sign of respect. People naturally like people who are like them. Whenever you are working with someone you don't know well, it's always a good idea to establish common ground with her. When you develop rapport through this method, it's easier to reach understanding.

Use this same method with your written communications. If you know that your receiver is a visual communicator, use visual words. If he's an auditory, it is more appropriate to use hearing type words. The same goes for kinesthetic people. A woman in my training class attended after her boss had completed the course. We knew he was an auditory communicator, but she didn't. She was visual in her style. She ran a branch of the bank and did not see him on a daily basis. Therefore, she wrote him many memos. All of her memos were written to a visual. He couldn't quite tune in to what she wanted. When she changed her style to match his, she was amazed how quickly they began communicating easily. She also got a promotion to vice president shortly after the class ended!

It's very simple. Remember, people like people who are like them. When you use this technique, you will be able to develop rapport with everyone almost instantly. Practice this tool daily and soon it will become second nature.

THE CONVERSATION STACK

When I started on my self-development journey several years ago, I found that my biggest difficulty came when I had to meet a new person. I didn't know what to say. I always felt uncomfortable and self-conscious. I could speak in front of a large group with no problem at all, but one-on-one conversations were a real chore. I learned a technique I think will make a difference for you too.

This is a memory technique, as well as a good way to start a conversation. It uses pictures and linking to help you carry on a conversation. Start at the bottom and work your way up:

7. **Jammed through the travellers checks is an opinion pole**

6. **Tucked in the pages of the book are hundreds of travellers checks**

5. **Stuck on the end of the skis is a large book**

4. **People are carrying long skis on their shoulders**

3. **Four people sitting on a horse—man, woman, two children**

2. **Large white work horse with long mane**

1. **Large name plate with name flashing in bright lights**

What does all this mean? Starting from the bottom, when we meet someone new, the name plate represents a question to ask the person: "What's your name?" When we are asking questions, the other person is doing the answering or talking. This makes it easy for us and we gain valuable information about them. The work horse represents the next question to ask, "What do you do for a living?" or "Where do you work?" The people represent a family, so ask, "Are you married?" or "Do you have kids?" The skis represent the question, "Do you have any hobbies?" The book represents the question, "Have you read anything good lately?" The travellers checks represent the question, "Have you taken a vacation recently?" or, "What was the best vacation you ever took?" And finally, the opinion pole represents the question, "What is your opinion on a current event?" (You may want to avoid politics and religion.)

When you use the conversation stack, practice mirroring and matching the other person as she answer your questions. As she is answering, you'll naturally begin to add your reactions intermittently. This is one of those simple little tools you can store away until you need it, then pull it out of your tool box.

UNDERSTANDING THE PEOPLE AROUND YOU

Another technology that will help you understand the people around you and help you understand yourself a little better is geometric psychology. This technology comes from right brain/left brain theory. As you know, the left brain is the more logical, rational, linear side of the brain. It's the more detailed, bottom-line oriented side. The right side is the more intuitive, emotional, global, and creative side of the brain.

This technology is considered public domain in the training industry. Many trainers and consultants use it as an icebreaker in sales or management training. It was expanded by Dr. Susan Dellinger in her book, *Psycho Geometrics.* I have used every behavior survey, from the simple to the highly complex (i.e. Myers-Briggs). Most are hard to understand and difficult to administer. Geometric psychology is as accurate as any, much simpler, and a lot more fun. Everyone with whom I share this can identify people around them immediately. Geometric psychology is fun and easy—so enjoy yourself as you learn more about you, and the people around you.

Look at the following five shapes. The triangle, square and rectangle are the more left-brained shapes with lots of angles and much more linear. The circle and the squiggly line are the more right-brained shapes, with no sharp angles, just round, flowing shapes. Look at these shapes and determine which one you are drawn to. You

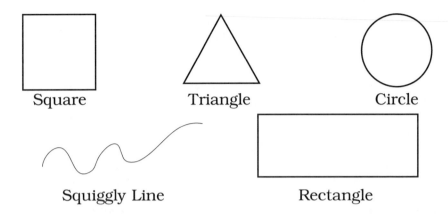

Square   Triangle   Circle

Squiggly Line   Rectangle

will like one of them more than the others. Keep this shape in mind.

Geometric psychology says that we are drawn to forms and shapes in our environment. Those shapes are reflected in our personalities through the clothes we wear, cars we drive, and the furniture we buy. Let's find out what each shape represents.

The **triangle** is the leadership symbol with the focus at the top. This personality style is very bottom-line oriented and wants to make things happen. The triangle is a global thinker, so don't bother her with details. The triangle will make things happen and get things done. Sometimes the triangle can be considered a little impatient, because he wants things to happen right now. The other down-side of the triangle is that he's working his way to the top, and doesn't really care whom he steps on to get there. It's always good to have a triangle on your team because he will keep everyone on task, seeing that the project gets completed on time.

The **box** or square is the very detail-oriented person. The box can't get enough details. Sometimes they're considered to be procrastinators because they're always looking for more information. Boxes are very organized individuals. Make sure you never move their things, as this will upset them. Boxes are great on a team because they will look for the details making sure that all the work is being done. Sometimes boxes are labeled as anti-social, because they don't want to be bothered with people, "Just the facts ma'am, just the facts."

The **rectangles** may seem to be a little confused and bewildered. This is only true because the rectangle is a transitional shape. This individual is moving from one shape to another. It is difficult to work for a rectangle because you never know how they will act. Rectangles are learning and growing, and will eventually settle down into a normal shape. Many times a person becomes a rectangle after a promotion or job change. Rectangles are very open to learning, they want as much new information as they can get. Don't despair, if you are a rectangle, you will settle into a "regular" shape eventually.

If you're a **circle,** you love people! The circle is the communication symbol. You love balance and harmony. Circles are the happy people who come to work singing and whistling. They will make sure that everyone gets to participate on your team. Be very careful with the circle though, when they go to lunch, they want to stay for three hours. The other downside of the circle is that they have a tendency to take on the mood of others. If they're talking with a depressed person, they can also become depressed. The circle is also a very detailed person. However, they don't collect facts and figures, they collect people details. Whenever you want to know about someone in your organization, ask a circle.

Finally, the **squiggly** line. This is the sexual and creative symbol. If you chose the squiggly line, you are sexually creative! The squiggly line has a very short attention span. It is hard to keep them on task. They have idea after idea. Some of these ideas may be considered a little outrageous. The squiggly line doesn't like structure. They don't want to be told to come to work at eight o'clock and leave at five o'clock. They're free spirited and want flexibility. It's important to have a squiggly line on your team. They'll generate lots and lots of creativity. Just don't expect them to like to stay on task as this cramps their style.

Typically, the triangle and the box get along quite well. The triangle loves to tell the box what to do. The triangle and the squiggly don't get along at all. The triangle will steal the squiggly's ideas and use them as their own. The circle and the box don't have a very good relationship, because the box doesn't want to be bothered with those people details... just let me get my job done. The circle and the squiggly will usually get along well, because the circle likes balance and they like to listen. The most dynamic leader will develop all three of these shapes. A triangle to get the job done, a circle to help them communicate effectively, and a squiggly to generate the creative ideas. The dynamic leader of the twenty-first century will look like this:

Charismatic Leader of the 90's

Knowing this about the shapes, did you pick the right one for yourself? About eighty percent of the people in our seminars stick with their first choice. It's important to realize that we all have a little of each of these shapes. It's also important to know that we change shapes as we learn, grow older, change jobs and relationships. Work on developing each of the shapes within yourself. This will help you get along better with others.

Typical Shapes and the Career Choices They Make

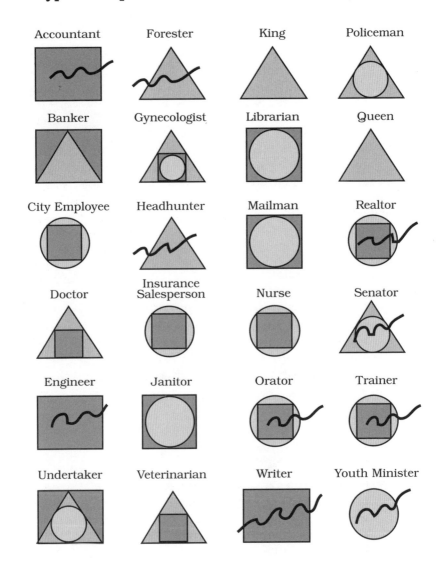

Accountant	Forester	King	Policeman
Banker	Gynecologist	Librarian	Queen
City Employee	Headhunter	Mailman	Realtor
Doctor	Insurance Salesperson	Nurse	Senator
Engineer	Janitor	Orator	Trainer
Undertaker	Veterinarian	Writer	Youth Minister

GETTING ALONG WITH EVERYONE

When I was growing up, I seemed to get along with everyone naturally (except my brothers, of course!). People used to make comments to me about being such a good listener and loyal friend. When I sat down to write this section, I decided to take stock of the attributes I have that made me, a circle, get along with everyone. You might find a lot of yourself in these attributes.

1. **Show empathy.** As a circle I find this comes very natural. It isn't feeling sorry for someone, it is simply identifying with their pain. To show empathy you might make a statement like, "You must feel terrible. I know I would if it had happened to me." This statement helps you to build rapport. When someone is down, you can't force them to cheer up. Gain rapport, and then you can ease them out of their pity party with some humor. Boxes and triangles will have a tough time with this tip. It feels unnatural to them, but with practice it will get easier.

2. **Be a good listener.** Again, this is a real circle trait. It is interesting for me to sit down and really listen to someone. And it is easy to see how important it makes them feel. Boxes really have to stretch to achieve this one. Especially if the conversation has anything to do with other people! Boxes want just the facts, just the facts.

3. **Create balance and harmony.** Smooth out the conflicts. Take it upon yourself to help others work through their problems. A savvy circle will make this happen without anyone realizing he did anything.

4. **Be assertive when necessary.** Asserting your rights and beliefs is positive. People will respect you for it. When you are passive, people simply push you around. When you are aggressive, people will avoid you. The assertive person goes for a win/win conclusion in every situation.

5. **Build trust as if your life depended on it.** Always follow through on commitments. If you say you will do something, do it. Always keep confidences. I was told something a long time ago, and I still live by it today. It is, Believe nothing that you hear, and only half of

what you see. When you don't make assumptions about others, you will probably not suffer assumptions made about you.

6. **Give credit away.** When you have been involved in a project and are receiving praise, make sure you share that praise with the people who helped you. Give credit to everyone who helped, not just a select few.

7. **Don't lie.** There is nothing worse than a liar. Make sure you are known as a person who is honest and trustworthy.

8. **Be congruent at all times.** To build and maintain credibility with others you have to walk the talk. Don't say one thing and do another. Dress, act, walk, and be consistent in your beliefs.

9. **Share compliments.** Even with strangers. You can always find something nice to say to someone. I stopped at a fast food restaurant to grab a soda on my way to a training session. As I walked past a woman she said, You look so pulled together and sharp. You really look nice. I thanked her and went on to my training session where I gave one of my best presentations ever!

10. **Don't whine!** I have a picture of one of my leadership classes with a participant standing in the middle of the picture, wearing a T-shirt. On the front of the shirt is a NO WHINING sign. I think these signs should be posted along the highways as a constant reminder for us all. Whining is irritating and boring. People will avoid you if you whine.

11. **Focus outward.** Don't worry about yourself, only concern yourself with the other person. What are they feeling, thinking, doing? How can I help them? Always keep your focus outward v. inward.

12. **Value differences.** This was tough for me until I got a little older. Where I was raised in southern Indiana everyone was of the same race, same national origin, and of like mind. I left that town thinking everyone had to be like me. When I went to work at Honeywell I had to adjust very quickly. We had every nationality, every race, and every temperament you could imag-

ine. It took a while, but now I realize how valuable those differences are.

BE A TEAM PLAYER

Today's business environment is flatter and leaner. Companies are instituting teams in order to maximize resources and responsiveness. Most managers spend fifty to ninety percent of their time working with internal or external teams. Teamwork has been called the third revolution in management. The old acronym T.E.A.M., of course, stands for, Together Everyone Achieves More. In order for you to fit into this new environment it's important for you to be a team player.

This is a list of team rules that I took from my son's little league team in 1975. I've adjusted it slightly for this application. If you follow them you will have no problem fitting into a team:

TEAM RULES

If it comes your way... handle it,

If you screw it up...admit it.

When you are tired...keep going,

When things aren't going well...keep trying.

When the boss speaks... pay attention,

When you lose... practice more,

When you win...be a good sport.

I was in charge of creating teamwork among a new directorate at Honeywell. We had five different departments brought together to form this new group. Eighty-eight people had to work together as a team and they didn't know each other. Many didn't like one another. Being a person who loves a challenge, I jumped right into this assignment.

We were implementing TQM, so we already had many programs set up to enhance the process. One program was called "Zero Defects Day." This was a day set aside by each department to recognize the importance of putting out quality products and for celebration of that success. I decided to bring all these employees together on that day to kick off our new TEAM. I organized a scavenger hunt. I divided all the employees into teams of eight or nine people, mixed up the departments so you had to work with someone new. No one was told what we were going to do, just that they were to meet in a certain room at a certain time.

When they were assembled into teams they were told to choose a leader, a co-leader and a name for their team. They were given a list of twenty items. I told them they could drive throughout Colorado Springs to find the items, being as creative as possible. The team with the most items would win and receive prizes. They had two hours. The list included a star and a snowman (it was summertime).

Creativity flowed. When the teams returned they had all kinds of items. Each team worked hard and had fun. Everyone learned something about the people they didn't know. Stories of the scavenger hunt lasted for months and people who hadn't worked well together were working smoothly on projects.

Some tips to help you build strong teams:

- **Be imaginative when building your teams**
- **Build trust among team members and yourself**
- **Help resolve conflict**
- **Learn to accept individual differences**
- **Get everyone involved in solving problems**
- **Give feedback and welcome the same**
- **Be supportive of other team member problems**
- **Communicate to build rapport**
- **Give respect and you will receive respect**
- **Get to know your team members; it will help you organize tasks to make the team more effective**
- **Never lie to your team members**
- **When you have bad news to share, share it quickly and answer all questions thoroughly**
- **Use humor to lighten a tense situation and make your teams open up**

Gender blending in teams is also very beneficial. Many men do not have the natural skills to be supportive and inspirational to other team members. Many women do not have the natural skills to build trust and communicate to command respect. When you blend the skills of each gender you create a dynamic leader who can inspire a team to greatness.

Even in unfortunate situations, team spirit can be built with a little wit and caring. At Honeywell we had a dynamic leader, Tom Mino. When the corporate executives told him he had to lay off hundreds of people he was upset, to say the least. So were the employees. Rumors started flying. Mino decided to use a tactic firefighters use to put out fires. Firefighters will start small fires to head off larger ones. He set up a flip chart outside of his office and called it the RUMOR BOARD. He told all of us that when we walked by the board we should write down all the rumors we'd heard, no matter how crazy. The flip chart filled up very quickly. Tom Mino was able to dispel the incorrect rumors and address the others head on.

Tom Mino had such strong leadership skills that he made everyone want to please him. I turned in my resignation in the middle of a critical cost proposal. I was supposed to leave around two o'clock on a Friday to head to Missouri. Instead I felt so loyal to Lewis Clark, my direct boss, and Tom Mino that I stayed until after six o'clock to finish the proposal. The following week, after I had arrived in Missouri and was instructing the movers where to place my furniture, I saw a flower truck pull up. The driver delivered a very large, beautiful house plant from Lewis Clark and Tom Mino with a note thanking me for my final support. I felt so good about myself after that. I never did get to thank them for the plant, so I will now. "THANKS!"

Human relation skills are part of the foundation for your success. To understand these interpersonal skills it's important to remember that whatever you give out is exactly what you get back. For instance—

> *There was a wise old gatekeeper watching over a large city surrounded by a wall. One day a weary traveler came up to the gatekeeper and asked, "We are looking for a new place to live. We are tired and need rest, can you tell me what kind of city this is?" The wise old gatekeeper stroked his beard and said, "Tell me what kind of a city you came from." The traveler said, "It was awful. Everyone stabbed each other in the back, they were all negative, and we hated it there." The gatekeeper thought for a moment and replied, "I'm afraid you'll find this city to be much the same." Soon another traveler came by the gatekeeper and said,*

*"We're looking for a new place to live. We're tired and
need rest, can you tell me what kind of city this is?"
The wise old gatekeeper stroked his chin and asked,
What kind of city did you come from? The traveler
smiled and said, "It was wonderful. Everyone helped
each other, and everyone was positive. We hated to
leave, but we had to." The gatekeeper smiled at the
traveler and replied, I think you'll find this city to be
much the same.*

Life is truly our mirror. Whatever we give out is exactly what we
receive in return. If you want trusting relationships, you must first be
trusting. I challenge you to watch what you are projecting to other people.

ACTION PAGE

The great aim of education is not
knowledge, but ACTION.
-Herbert Spencer

ACTION STEPS
To High Performance

The major benefit I gained from this chapter was:

_____

_____

_____

_____

Based on this benefit, my High Performance Action Plan is:

_____

_____

_____

_____

Why is this action plan important to me?

_____

_____

_____

_____

Section 3

The Inclination

"When you have a bent toward doing or accomplishing something, then you are inclined to make it happen. In this section the powers are your desire to move forward. These powers ignite the spark that is within you."

Chapter 7

Positive Attitude: A Personal Empowerment Model

Attitudinize...strike a positive mental attitude, then don't let anyone or anything drag you down.
- Cheri Swales Bair

As Grandma Moses said, "Life is what we make it, always has been, always will be." We can make our lives positive and fruitful or negative and dismal. High Performers always choose the positive. That's what power number four is all about—Positive Attitude: a Personal Empowerment Model.

I work with many individuals who are hard-working achievers. They believe in everything surrounding the High Performance Success System. Typically they don't believe they're ever negative or judgmental. Believe me, all of us have had a time when we have made a negative statement to ourselves. Maybe for you it's when you're playing golf and hit a bad shot, or when you're in a hurry and remember that you left the iron on and you slip and say to yourself. "Way to go Cheri," or "That was dumb." It's important to pay attention to these little negatives, because they build into big negatives.

I'm not suggesting that you should never be negative or feel down. I'm simply saying that high performance people realize they are human and will have a complete array of feelings. It's okay to feel down or negative—just don't stay there! Build a positive attitude that allows you to bounce back quickly from any negative situation.

ATTITUDE CHECKLIST

Here's a short attitude check. Just answer "yes" or "no" to each of the following questions:

1. **Do you like yourself?**

2. **Do you work to become a better you?**

3. **Do you set goals and work to achieve them daily?**

4. **Do you look at problems as opportunities?**

5. **Are you open to learning?**

6. **Are you willing to listen?**

7. **Are you a considerate person?**

8. **Do you take risks?**

9. **Do you take responsibility for your feelings and actions?**

10. **Do you smile often?**

11. **Are you usually in a good mood?**

12. **Do you enjoy your life?**

If you answered YES to all of these questions, you have a positive mental attitude. If you answered NO to any of these questions, it's time to start working on your attitude!

Since the sixties, when psychologists began focusing on the effects of a positive mental attitude, I've read every book and listened to every tape about this topic that I could get my hands on. What I found consistently are five major points to understand about your attitude:

First: Your attitude is the way you see your environ ment.

Second: Your attitude is formed from your perception of what you see in your world.

Third: You have control over your attitude.

**Fourth: You can turn a negative attitude into a
positive attitude.**

Fifth: Your positive attitude is a priceless possession.

NEGATIVE FACTORS

Several years ago, I read a book by James T. McCay called, *The Management of Time*. In this book he talks about negative factors. He says that negative factors drag us down and create energy leaks. Many of the negative attitudes he pointed out were typical issues we run into at home and work: defensiveness, criticism, resentment, suspicion, fear, worry, and contempt. He wrote that negatives usually come in clusters like aphids (plant parasites). And if you develop one, you'll soon have a thriving colony.

These negative factors will breed and deplete energy very rapidly. Below is a diagram he used which shows the relationship between negative factors, your energy, and how energy decreases rapidly when negative factors are introduced.

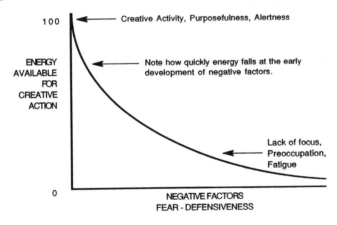

**(Reprinted from the book *The Management of Time*, James T. McCay, 1959,
1987. Used with permission of the publisher, Prentice Hall/A Division of Simon
& Schuster, Englewood Cliffs, N. J.)**

When you develop a positive attitude toward life, you become empowered. Things start going right for you. You are able to recognize possibilities and opportunities. You also attract positive, energetic and happy people to you. You tend to become highly motivated and effective. In turn, this increases your ability to make things happen.

IMPROVE YOUR ATTITUDE

Here are some tips for developing a positive attitude that I have used throughout my life:

SMILE! We usually smile when we feel good, and that makes sense. Our face is showing how we feel internally. Research done by the School of Medicine at the University of California at San Francisco in the early 80's shows that this information is transmitted both ways. You can make yourself feel bad by frowning or you can make yourself feel good (positive) by smiling. It's very difficult to smile and feel rotten at the same time. Go ahead, try it, smile and try to think negative thoughts. It just won't work!

Another way to improve your attitude is to develop a strong network of friends. When you get down or upset, call a friend who you know will help you feel better. Everyone has someone who makes them feel good. Maybe it isn't someone you can call, maybe it is someone who wrote a book or made history and you admire them. Just pick up a book and read about them and imagine what they would tell you. When I get down, I call my friend Donna, because she always says the right things to make me feel good.

You can also take a walk in the park or on a nature trail. As you're walking, breath deeply and smell the fresh air. Listen to the birds sing. You'll feel great! Go for a run or work out at the gym. Play some racquetball or tennis. Just get busy. Idleness and boredom allow the negatives to start creeping into the mind. Generate activity and positivity follows.

My favorite way of lifting my spirits is to put on my favorite music. No matter what you are doing, you can listen to your favorite music. You know, the kind that makes you want to sing along and tap your foot. Every time my husband Tom wants to feel really good, he plays his favorite oldies from the 60's and 70's. These are very strong anchors for him. It doesn't matter what kind of music it is, as long as it makes you feel good. When I have to complete a chore that I'm not overly fond of doing, like cleaning the bathroom, I'll get out my favorite Roger Whitaker album. I love his music so much, I usually end up cleaning longer, just to continue listening to my favorite music. It's not uncommon for people to tell me that they saw me singing and rocking in my car while I was waiting at a stop light. Hey—it's fun, and when you're having fun, you're building your positive attitude.

It used to be very difficult for me to get out of bed in the morning. The bed was nice and warm, and it just felt good to lie there. I would turn the alarm off every ten minutes for about a half an hour. You know how that can be. Maybe your job just doesn't excite you any more, or you just don't like your boss, or maybe you lost your job. It becomes tough to crawl out of a nice secure bed to face what we tell ourselves is going to be a rotten day. Well, that's just it—it's what we TELL ourselves. We can talk ourselves into almost anything, like a headache or being tired, or even being unhappy or lonely. What I suggest is that as you wake up each morning, just about the time you start becoming aware of your consciousness, start making positive statements in your mind. "Today is going to be a great day," "I love my job," "I can't wait to get going," "Life is wonderful!" You'll be amazed how quickly it will become fact. If you think this is stretching the truth, don't worry. Your subconscious mind doesn't know the difference between fact and fiction. In no time you'll start hopping right out of bed in the morning, energized and ready to go.

Become a master reframer. Turn every negative into a positive. For instance, if you didn't get the job you wanted, reframe that into, "I'll be more prepared for the next opportunity," or "There will be a better opportunity soon." I learned this technique from a very good friend several years ago. Emma would always find the silver lining. One time I told her I had lost an assignment because of a mistake I'd made. She picked up the phone to make a call and I asked, "What are you doing?" "I'm calling a friend of mine who is always looking for positive, intelligent people who learn from their mistakes," Emma said. Learn to reframe situations to the positive and you're well on your way to success.

CHOOSE TO BE HAPPY! Find something to appreciate. I find this so easy to do, simply by appreciating the many inspirational and wondrous things in life. I was driving to the post office in our downtown area recently. As I came to a stoplight I noticed a young woman in a wheelchair who was obviously seriously handicapped. She was having difficulty maneuvering her wheelchair across the intersection. Even with her difficulties, she never faltered or asked for help. She kept going until she made it across the street. I was so inspired that tears came to my eyes as I reflected on the good fortune of having a happy healthy family. You come across inspirational people every day; you just have to be watching for them.

A woman who attended a High performance Training Course, is now a dear friend. She had polio as a child. Her legs are crippled, but she walks everywhere without even a cane for support. I know that much of the time she is in great pain, yet she smiles and exudes a wonderful positive attitude. And you know, it isn't just her determination that inspires me, it's the fact that she doesn't consider or perceive herself as handicapped. When you become aware of the many inspirational people with whom you come into contact, you can't help but feel happy and positive.

Another tip that I gained several years ago was to develop the belief that everything happens for a reason.

When you develop this belief and program it into your mind-computer and keep it stored there, you'll be able to retrieve it whenever you need it. After the break up of my first marriage I kept dwelling on the fact that I must not have been a good wife. Until my boss told me that everything happens for a reason. Even through all the negative in this marriage and its subsequent demise, I realized how much better I would be in a new relationship. I really had learned a lot from this negative situation. This belief has helped me get through many tough spots in my life and I share it with everyone, because it is so valuable.

Another graduate, Linda, told how she and her staff at work tend to feed off each other's attitude. She said they caught themselves **AWFULIZING**. The more one person felt sorry for themselves, or imagined horrible things, the more the whole group jumped in to AWFULIZE. She said once they recognized what they were doing, they were able to stop AWFULIZING!

Everyone has a special way of building a positive attitude. We have so many inspiring individuals who go through our training classes. I'd like to tell you about a few: One man came to class one evening with a small file box. He said it was his box of positives. Everything good he receives, he places it, or something that represents it, in his positive box. Whenever he's down, he just looks through his box of positives for a boost. A woman in our training brought in a collage representing her goals. She clipped out several pictures representing her goals from old magazines and glued them onto poster board. Whenever she needed a boost, she just looked at her goal poster to remember what she was shooting for. Another woman in one of our classes had a very special picture taken. She put on her favorite business outfit and had someone snap a close-up picture of her smiling a great big smile. She had several copies of this picture made and put one in her briefcase, one in her desk drawer, and one on her vanity mirror. Everywhere she goes she can see herself as a powerful, positive person! Use any or all of these techniques for yourself. Just modify them to fit your circumstances and enjoy!

ATTITUDINIZE

Finally, I challenge you to **ATTITUDINIZE!** STRIKE AN ATTITUDE and become an unshakable optimist. Absolutely refuse to look at the negative. Look for the BEST in EVERY person you meet. Read about people who inspire you. Listen to audio tapes relentlessly and attend motivational seminars. Hang around positive people and discuss positive topics. And always look for good things happening in your company and your life. ATTITUDINIZE and don't let anyone or anything drag you down. Here are twenty-six steps to ATTITUDINIZE and maintain it:

1. **Change your self talk.** Listen to yourself. Approximately seventy-five percent of what we say to ourselves is negative. Think the word STOP in your mind to shut down negative thoughts.

2. **Take a positive snapshot of yourself.** Keep this fun picture somewhere close so you see it often.

3. **Hang around positive people.** Avoid the NIOP's (negative input of other people).

4. **Get a pet.** Animals can be very soothing, and they will love you no matter what!

5. **Present a professional image.** When you look professional, you feel better and your attitude is more positive.

6. **Exhibit enthusiasm for yourself and others.** People want to be around enthusiastic people—not boring, low power people.

7. **Do nice things for people.** Kind deeds are a good way to make yourself feel good. Give without expectation and your positive attitude will strengthen.

8. **Take attitude breaks.** Get away from stress and pressure by taking a brisk walk and smelling the fresh air whenever you can.

9. **Keep track of your successes.** Not just big ones! Make a note if you stick to your diet or complete your to do list. It helps to eliminate that I haven't accomplished anything feeling.

10. **Share compliments.** Let friends, family and co-workers know they've done a good job. Make sure you are sincere.

11. **Capitalize on your strengths.** Know your strengths and play them up. If you have superior people skills, make sure you use them. Doing what you're good at is an easy way to feel positive.

12. **Organize yourself.** It's difficult to be positive when you are scattered and disorganized. Pull it all together and you will feel great and get more done.

13. **Take time for yourself.** When you take time to be alone you can renew yourself and filter out the negatives in your life.

14. **Believe in yourself completely.** Know that you are the best you can be and never stop growing and changing.

15. **Make positive affirmations.** Write out positive statements and say them over and over to yourself. Don't stop this when you begin to feel better. Keep it up with a passion.

16. **Avoid giving excuses.** Many times being defensive is simply giving excuses. This is one of those negative factors.

17. **Choose to be physically healthy.** When your body feels good your mind and emotions will follow.

18. **Develop a sense of humor.** Look at the light side and laugh often. Any situation has a humorous side if you just take the time to look at it from a different perspective.

19. **Learn from your mistakes.** In life there are losers and there are learners. Make sure you learn from everyone and everything.

20. **Teach others to be positive.** When you teach, you learn. Help others develop a bright outlook and yours will become even brighter.

21. **Read an inspirational book.** Find a story that inspires you and read it. Find one that you can really identify with, and your positive feelings will flow.

22. **Hang motivational posters on your walls.** When you look at them you'll feel better immediately. Others will enjoy them too.

23. **Stand up for yourself.** When you are assertive you will feel strong, and your positive attitude grows.

24. **Imagine yourself positive.** Visualize yourself as a

happy, optimistic, positive person and you will become that person.

25. Nurture your creativity. When you tap into your creative problem-solving skills, you'll be able to solve more issues, and each time you feel better.

26. Throw yourself a pity party! Go off by yourself and yell or stomp around. Tell yourself all the bad things about yourself and get it all out of your system. Make it short and powerful and then get on with things.

We all have a very positive person inside of us. All we have to do is to reach inside and let them out. Here's a story that explains what I mean.

*There once was a baby Bengal tiger who, shortly after birth, was separated from his mother. Somehow, he ended up living with a herd of goats. The little Bengal tiger did everything that the kids did. He played goat games and nursed with the other kids. One day a great big Bengal tiger came into the field where the goats lived. As he entered all of the goats scattered. But, for some reason the little Bengal tiger stayed. The big tiger looked down at the little one and ROARED— "Don't you know that you are a mighty Bengal tiger? What are you doing here with a bunch of goats? Let me hear you ROAR like a tiger!" The little Bengal tiger mustered up what he could and said, "Roar". The big tiger said, Come on, you can do it, really let me hear it! The baby tiger said, "Roar." The big tiger said, "Come on, really let me hear it, like this, ROAR!" The baby tiger hunkered down and gave it all he could and let out a big, **ROARRRR!** "Now, said the Big Bengal Tiger, you don't have to be a goat any more!"*

We all have a very noble creature inside of us. I challenge you to reach down inside yourself and find that positive attitude. Live up to your nobility, not just your ability.

ACTION PAGE

The great aim of education is not knowledge, but ACTION.
-Herbert Spencer

ACTION STEPS
To High Performance

The major benefit I gained from this chapter was:

_____

_____

_____

_____

Based on this benefit, my High Performance Action Plan is:

_____

_____

_____

_____

Why is this action plan important to me?

_____

_____

_____

_____

Chapter 8

Peace of Mind: The High Performance State

*Stress: The condition we experience when the brain
overrides the body's urge to choke the living ?@! out of
some ?@! who we think really deserves it.*
Anonymous

- **95,000,000 Americans suffer from tension related to physical or psychological problems.**

- **70 to 90% of all medical problems are stress related.**

- **Lower back pain is the leading cause of work-related disabilities.**

Peace of mind: The High Performance State is the fifth power in the High Performance Model. Sounds wonderful, doesn't it? Every day we're faced with change, pressure, commitments, deadlines, and other stress inducing situations. These situations are not going to go away. Our information base is doubling every five years, it's up to us to find ways to achieve peace of mind. We can become stress captains navigating our way through the stream of changes causing stress. We can even use stress to our benefit.

How does stress manifest in your body? Everyone experiences stress in different ways: headaches, stomach problems, neck and back pain, feeling tired, and other minor physical problems. Mentally we have confusion, sleep disorders, forgetfulness, anxiety, fear, depression, and anger. All of these can cause serious illness, and lower productivity resulting from a high rate of absenteeism.

Many techniques taught for several years can help you control stress and overcome tension. I believe the best thing you can do is to re-learn these skills frequently, continuing to look for new technical skills, remaining open to all new avenues. You can become stress captains navigating your way through your sea of stressors.

I'm going to provide you with several techniques that will help you control stress and develop peace of mind. Some of these techniques will require you to close your eyes or make specific movements. Use the techniques that work best for you. I recommend that you read this chapter when you have access to a private and quiet area where you will not be interrupted.

STRESSOR SURVEY

Here is a list of potential stressors. Follow the instructions to determine your level of stress. Look over the list below deciding which items apply to you. Then rate each item you have chosen from 1 to 100, with 100 being the most severe. (The stressors you choose should be applicable within the past year.) Put the number on each line. Add all the numbers to determine your stressor score.

ITEM

Death of spouse	___	Death of child	___
Break up of relationship	___	Being robbed	___
Being assaulted	___	Family arguments	___
Mild illness	___	Serious illness	___
Dislike job	___	Rush hour traffic	___
Disagreements with friends	___	Unpleasant boss	___
Inflation	___	Recession	___
Being unemployed	___	Uncooperative staff	___
Visiting the dentist	___	Social obligations	___
Gaining weight	___	Being in school	___
Someone close is ill	___	Planning a vacation	___
Changing a habit	___	Getting married	___

Losing weight	____	Having a baby	____
Being fired	____	Hot weather	____
Moving	____	Getting older	____
Visiting the doctor	____	Interviewing	____
Auto breakdown	____	Cold weather	____
Death of a loved one	____	Having a party	____
Child leaving home	____	Appliance breakdown	____
Business meetings	____	Promotion	____
Large investment	____	Large debt	____
New hobby	____	Boredom	____
Too much work	____	Retirement	____
Travel	____	Other	____

TOTAL: ____

As you complete this survey keep in mind that one person's stressor is another person's energizer. The rule of thumb for this survey is that if your total is 300 or more, you need to do something about the stress in your life. Maybe taking a stress reduction class or reading a book. It might even be eliminating the particular stressor from your life.

When my husband and I moved to Missouri in 1990, I took this survey. My score was 3,598! I was having back pain so severe I could hardly get out of bed in the morning. Here are the things that were happening in my life at the time: Honeywell had decided to sell our division. I decided to make a career change. My oldest son, who is significantly older than our other children, decided to live with us. We took three vacations. Tom's father, who has had a stroke, came for an extended visit. We were unable to sell our house before our move. I had to give away Moose, my basset hound. Tom moved to Missouri four months before I could. Fortunately, many of these things were self-inflicted, and I could make easy changes. Stress is many times a choice. We simply need to make the right choices.

SWITCHING ON YOUR WHOLE BRAIN

Roger Sperry's work in the early 70's gave us much understanding of the brain. From his research we learned that there are indeed two distinct sides of the brain. As High Performers we want to make sure that we are using both sides of our brain—our whole brain, for a change. This research has helped us to make great strides in learning effectively. Out of right brain/left brain theory has come a technology called Educational Kinesiology developed by Dr. Paul Dennison and his wife Gail. The idea behind educational kinesiology is that we tend to get locked in one side of the brain and we really need better hemispheric integration. Typically, as professionals in a very bottom-line oriented world, we get locked in our left or "try" brain. This can cause even more stress and tension for us. You see this at work every day when you watch people walking down the hall. They will very often have their hands in their pockets or swinging at their sides, but never crossing the mid-line of the body. EK tells us that we have an imaginary mid-line that runs down the middle of our bodies and in order to switch-on both sides of the brain we must physically cross that midline. This movement creates electrochemical impulses that cause the switching-on effect. Dr. Paul Dennison and his wife Gail share several exercises in their books *Brain Gym* and *Edu-K for Kids*. What we have found is that these exercises are very helpful for professionals. Here are some exercises from *Brain Gym*.

COOK'S HOOK-UP

The first technique is called the Cook's Hook-up. The Cook's Hook-up will help you immediately release stress and tension. Sit down in a straight backed chair. Get comfortable, crossing your ankles on the floor in front of you. Put your hands straight out in front of you, with the backs of your hands touching. Bring your right wrist up over your left wrist so that the palms of your hands are touching. Clasp your fingers together lightly. With your hands clasped together move your hands downward, bringing your elbows out to each side, allowing your hands to be pulled back up through your arms. Rest your clasped hands on your chest. Hold this position for three or four minutes. Take deep breaths as you sit in the Cook's Hook-up, relaxing your jaw muscle. Slowly you'll feel the tension dissipate as you are integrating both hemispheres of the brain. Any time that you feel stressed out, simply go to a quiet place where you will not be inter-

Cook's Hook-up

Use the Cook's hook-up to "switch-on" your whole brain. This exercise will help you control stress almost instantly. It doesn't take long, so find a quiet spot for about 3-5 minutes and access your peace of mind.

rupted and sit in the Cook's Hook-up for just a few minutes. When you are finished you feel refreshed and ready to go.

CROSS CRAWL

Another technique to help switch on your whole brain allowing you to become more alert and less stressed, is the Cross Crawl. Basically the Cross Crawl is the process of crawling while you are standing up. Touch your left wrist to your right knee, crossing the mid-line with your arms and legs. Then, the right wrist to the left knee. Once you have the motion it isn't necessary to continue touching . . . just do the movement. Do the Cross Crawl about twenty times. Now stop and go through the homolateral march, raising the same leg and the same arm at the same time. This is like a toy soldier marching, very methodical. Do this to a count of twenty. Which one felt better to you? If you are a fairly whole brained person, the cross crawl probably felt less tiring and more fluid. If you are strong in your dom-

Cross Crawl

Use the cross crawl to "switch-on" your whole brain. This exercise will help you to wake up and be more alert and productive. Make sure you are crossing the midline of the body with your hands and knees. Continue for a count of twenty, and you'll be ready to go!

inance of the left brain, then the homolateral march was probably the best for you. We want to repattern your brain so that the cross crawl has you switched-on. Do the Cross Crawl again.

OTHER OPTIONS TO HELP YOU DEAL WITH STRESS

Here are some additional tips for navigating stress successfully:

1. Develop a technique for **relaxing your muscles.** Relaxing the muscles helps us become aware of the tension we hold in different parts of our bodies. I'll share a technique with you at the end of this section that will help you relax almost instantly.

2. State **positive affirmations** into your subconscious mind. When we constantly make statements like, I'm afraid, or I am lonely, we are proving these through our subconscious. Reframe those to state, I live a happy, fearless life.

3. Develop **realistic goals and a pattern of success.** When we set goals that are too high for us to attain, we constantly face failure. Set goals that are attainable and you will start seeing successes.

4. Rely on your **religious convictions.** When all else fails, give your worries to a higher power. Don't think that you are all alone.

5. Develop a **sense of control.** One way to do this is to do what one graduate of our course does. Muriel says, "Don't sweat the small stuff," and then she adds, "Everything's the small stuff."

6. Use **humor, laughter and playing.** Any time you can take a tense situation and use some humor to lighten the moment, you relieve stress and tension. Have some fun and just laugh. Remember—five years from now who's going to care anyway?

7. Add **variety** to your life and to your job. Some times just doing repetitive and tedious tasks over and over can be stressful. Do things a little differently and give yourself a break!

8. Take a **one-minute vacation.** In your mind visualize your special place. Go there and enjoy, even if it's for just a minute.

9. Rethink your **priorities.** Many times we create extra stress for ourselves simply by having the wrong priorities. Evaluate what is important to you right now and see if your priorities change.

10. Use the technique of **massage.** Either have your spouse or a professional masseuse give you a massage. This can be a very relaxing experience and beneficial for your overall health.

11. **Pet your dog or cat.** Animals can be the most cuddly creatures. You'll feel the anxiety run out of your body. I like to sit and gaze at an aquarium full of tropical fish; it's very soothing.

12. Improve your **physical health.** Avoid caffeine, sugar, cholesterol, nicotine, salt, alcohol, smog and other chemicals that have been found to increase stress.

13. **Exercise regularly.** You don't have to become a hard core health fanatic; however, you do need to avoid being a couch potato. Get out and walk. Walk during lunch, before or after work. Walking is great for the heart and releasing anxiety and tension.

14. Become a **"no limit" person.** Understand that you can do anything that you want, if you want to badly enough. Restrictions and limits are stress inducers.

15. **Give hugs.** People need to be touched. Give hugs and see how much better you feel.

16. **Get used to stress in your body** so you can identify your reactions to it quickly. One way is to notice where your tongue is at any given moment. If it is pushed against the roof of your mouth, you are having stress.

17. **Take charge of yourself** and forget about taking charge of others. Don't insist that everyone agree. Stop feeling responsible for everyone else.

18. Be **accepting.** Tolerance and understanding will go a long way in eliminating your stress level.

19. Be **in touch with life**, living it fully. Be in the present and let go of the past. Remain alert and aware of yourself, and your situation, constantly learning new and creative ways to cope with stressors.

20. Live **one day at a time.** Dale Carnegie says, "Live in day tight compartments."

21. Maintain a strong **network of friends.** In times of need, friends are your greatest resource.

22. Use a **biofeedback device** like biodots. Biodots are small circles you place on the back of your hand which change color based on your skin temperature and the level of your stress. (Order biodots by calling 1-800-383-6919.)

23. Learn to **give in to the things** that are really unimportant to you.

24. Don't talk about your **negatives.**

25. Be open to **feedback** from others.

TIPS FROM HIGH PERFORMERS

These are just a few of the techniques that people have shared in High Performance Training. A tip came from Steve. He said that when he is facing a particularly bad time in his life, he simply looks at it like reading a book. Steve says, "I'm skipping that chapter." Another participant said that she collects stressors during the day, ending up with a full bucket at day's end. All she does is dump her bucket when she leaves work. Frank treats stress like a hearing test. He imagines putting on a set of headphones. As the beeps get lower and lower, so does his stress level. One other tip from a graduate is every time she becomes stressed out, she asks herself what her favorite cartoon character would do. She has a good laugh and lowers her stress level.

This tip comes from another participant in my training, Donna. She taught me a self-hypnosis technique. Donna is auditory, when sharing this technique, her gentle, fluid tonality was very relaxing. Here's how it goes:

Relax in a quiet place. In your mind, think of three things you can see, then think of three things you can hear, then think of three things you can feel. Next, think of two things you can see, then think of two things you can hear, and two things you can feel. Last, think of one thing you can see, one thing you can hear, and one thing you can feel. Relax completely and make a positive statement to yourself about what you want to happen. Maybe your statement is to go to sleep, or to become healthier, or to become more confident.

MUSCLE RELAXATION TECHNIQUE

You may have done something like this in the past. If so, try it again using visualization to enhance the exercise. This is a relaxation exercise and some "mind" gymnastics. Close your eyes. Take a couple of deep breaths, feeling tension drain away from your body as you exhale. You will be experiencing a tool that can help you release stress almost instantly. Starting with your toes, you will be flexing (tightening) then releasing different muscles in your body. Now flex your toes, hold them tightly, then release. Flex your calves. Feel them tightening, then release. Flex your thighs, hold them, then release. Flex your buttocks, release; your stomach, release; your lower back, release; your chest, release; your hands, release; your arms, release. Tighten your shoulders by raising them up as far as they can go, release; tighten your neck, release and roll it a couple of times feeling the tension release. Make a face, stick out your tongue, hold it, release dropping and relaxing your jaw muscles. We hold a lot of tension in our jaw muscle, let it go. Picture a stop sign. Bring it right up in front of your face. Now move it away from your face. Make it bigger, as big as the room. Shrink it down to normal size. Turn it green. Make it red again. Cut it in half. Put it back together. Shrink it down to postage stamp size and throw it over your right shoulder. Picture a treehouse. Your treehouse from your childhood, or the one you wish you'd had. Put yourself in the treehouse. Look around. What do you see, hear, feel? Do you hear birds singing? Can you feel the warm summer breeze against your face? Shrink yourself to six inches tall. Look around you. What do you see? Return to your normal size enjoying the relaxing feeling of your own special hide-away. When you are ready, open your eyes.

We can choose to be in charge of the movies of our minds learning to relax and develop peace of mind. We can talk ourselves into stress and anxiety or we can accept peace of mind and live happy lives.

BECOME A CHANGE MASTER

Tom Peters tells us to become change agents. You can become a change master and handle all the changes that occur around you. As I said earlier, our life is merely a cycle of change. Here are some tips for handling change and transitions:

- **Control your attitude!**

- **Be tolerant of others' mistakes**

- **Look for change, expect change, create change**

- **Avoid blaming others for the change**

- **Don't blame all your problems on the change**

- **Be prepared for psychological pain and grieving**

- **Develop a network of friends you can turn to for support**

- **Look at the change as an opportunity to grow and develop**

- **Use humor**

- **Don't stop living or doing your job**

It is very important for us to realize what we are programming into our subconscious mind because our actions tend to follow our thoughts. Like my husband, Tom, always says, Watch what you say to yourself, it will come true. A few years ago, my brother David and I flew back to Indiana to attend our father and step-mother's retirement party. On the flight back to Indiana, he told me about one of his employees at his insurance agency. David was really concerned because his employee's mother had died recently and he hadn't been coping well with her death. Before we left Colorado, his employee had been put in the hospital for testing. We returned to Colorado three days later and his employee had died. It was a case of this man literally killing himself with his mind. He couldn't cope and programmed into his mind/computer that there was nothing to live for. That became his reality.

Another story about people programming and becoming their reality comes from another graduate, Michelle. She missed one of the training sessions because she went to her grandmother's eightieth birthday party. The next day, her grandmother died. Michelle shared that her grandmother had always made the statement that she just wanted to live to be eighty. She was healthy, strong and happy at her birthday party. The next day she passed away. She lived up to her own expectations.

GENDER-BLENDING AND STRESS CONTROL

When it comes to stress, gender-blending is critical. Women worry about anything and everything. Men, on the other hand, worry only about the BIG problems. Women will release much of their stress through crying and talking with friends. Men stuff as many stressors into their mind/computer as possible.

Women need to step back and stop worrying about the things that are out of their control. Men need to learn to cry and release some of the fear and anger they have bottled up inside.

This isn't easy for the sexes to do. We have to work at gender-blending and gain the best from each other.

Here's a final story that sums it all up:

> A railroad yard worker was checking cars right before quitting time and he accidentally got locked in a refrigerator car. There was no safety latch inside the car. No one could hear his cries for help. He sat down on a box and tried to figure out what to do. He knew that he would freeze to death, so he began writing the symptoms he experienced on a piece of scrap paper. "I am shivering, I am getting colder, I am beginning to feel numb—" until his writing became illegible. The next day his body was found by his coworkers. The results of the autopsy were that he had frozen to death. When they checked the railroad car they found that it had been turned off. The temperature in the railroad car was 55 degrees. The power of the mind, and his belief that he was in a refrigerator car, caused his death.

We must control what our subconscious tapes are telling us. We truly create our own destiny. Our perception creates our reality. I challenge you to reprogram your subconscious mind and begin changing your old limiting belief system. Become a stress captain and navigate your stress into success!

ACTION PAGE

The great aim of education is not knowledge, but ACTION.
-Herbert Spencer

ACTION STEPS
To High Performance

The major benefit I gained from this chapter was:

_____

_____

_____

_____

Based on this benefit, my High Performance Action Plan is:

_____

_____

_____

_____

Why is this action plan important to me?

_____

_____

_____

_____

Chapter 9

Personal Balance: Controlling Your World

To everything there is a season....and a time for every
purpose under the heavens
Ecclesiastes 3:1

A man once built up a tremendous fortune. He worked long hours and had a difficult time clearing his mind of work. After several years his wife grew tired of his lack of attention toward her, so she left him and took his fortune. The man became very lonely after awhile so he took another wife. Again he worked hard and he rebuilt his fortune. And again, his wife felt lonely and neglected and she, too, left and took his fortune. Once again, in his loneliness, the man remarried and began rebuilding his fortune. He worked until he was exhausted every day. His third wife left him and again, took his fortune. A very persistent man, he remarried one more time and had to rebuild his fortune. He did this by working very hard every day. And yes, you guessed right. His fourth wife left him and took his fortune. This is a true story. Obviously, this man didn't understand the importance of personal balance.

Personal Balance: Controlling Your World, is Power six in the High Performance Success System. It is also the most important power in the model. Personal balance can be the *toughest* to achieve, yet it yields the greatest rewards. Personal balance cannot be forced, financed or faked, it simply comes from understanding.

PERSONAL BALANCE (NOT TIME MANAGEMENT)

Please, don't confuse personal balance with time management. I tell people that there's no such thing as time management. You have no control over time. There are sixty seconds in a minute, sixty minutes in an hour, and twenty-four hours in a day. You have no control over that. What you do have control over is what you do with your 86,400 seconds in each day. I'm always amazed at the participants in our training who tell me how they have gained time management skills. What they have really gained is an understanding of self-management! Self-management is gaining a new perspective on who you are and what you want in life. It is a total understanding that we are a part of a much greater system. This understanding will allow us to have everything fall into place, naturally.

When I talk about personal balance, I'm referring to the understanding that you are a total person, not just a professional, not just a spouse, but a whole, unique individual. Personal balance consists of three specific areas for every individual: the mental area, the physical area, and the spiritual area. Understanding the real meaning of personal balance is very important to every High Performer. Think of your own personal balance like a tripod for a camera. In order for the camera to take clear, focused pictures and work effectively, the tripod must be balanced. Each of the three legs of the tripod must be set at equal lengths in order for the tripod to be balanced. If the tripod is out of balance, the pictures from the camera might be unfocused or off center. It's much the same for you and me. If you are not balanced mentally, physically and spiritually, you will not perform at your highest level, consistently.

You work on balance and don't even realize it. You're balancing things all day long. You balance your checkbook, your tires, and your diet. You even balance the chlorine in your swimming pool and the weights on your fishing line! And you make attempts at balancing the national budget! Watch a golfer go through specific balancing mechanics to perfect his golf swing. The golfer will balance his weight evenly between his feet when he addresses the ball. As he goes into his back swing, his balance shifts to his back foot. As he swings down and through the ball, his center of balance transfers from his back foot to his front foot. We go to all the trouble to balance all these external things. Don't you think it's time to balance yourself?

NATURAL LAWS

Much of my discussion on personal balance stems from information from the martial arts and from nature.

They have helped me to understand the importance of personal balance. I have also gained a lot from how the simple things in life are balanced. There are three natural laws that I would like to share with you. Understanding these laws will help you achieve personal balance. It's important to understand there are some things which are out of our control. Knowing them allows you to focus on the items that are within your control. This will help you to gain personal balance more easily.

I was raised in southern Indiana in a very rural setting, surrounded by farmers. As a small girl I would watch my grandmother plant her garden in the spring and I couldn't wait until fall to taste the plump, juicy tomatoes and devour the huge, fleshy lima beans. I learned from this that everything has a beginning and an end. You plant the seeds, and they grow into mature vegetables that are harvested and eaten. Needless to say, my favorite seasons of the year are spring and fall. This is the law of natural progression. Everything and everyone develops and grows with time. When you speed up the process, you are trying too hard. This creates blockages. When you follow the natural progression of things and do your best, you fall easily into balance. The same happens when you are trying too hard at work or at home. The brain gets switched off, and you are unbalanced.

LAW ONE. THE LAW OF NATURAL PROGRESSION tells us that there exists a natural progression over time. Certain things in life cannot be rushed due to the law of progression. Like the growing of vegetables and growing from a child to an adult. You can't change the fact that summer follows spring and winter follows fall, nor can you change or rush any natural process without causing imbalance.

When I was in my early twenties I remember looking to advance my career. I wanted to be and thought I should be the president of the company where I worked. I learned a good lesson from a gentleman I worked with at that company. He always took everything in stride. I thought of him as too laid back. He looked at me one day as I was rushing around to make things happen and he said in his low, slow voice, "Cheri, patience is a virtue. You could use some patience." As a High Performer when you develop patience, natural progression is easier to accept. When you accept natural progression, personal balance is easier to attain and success follows.

This is the most difficult law to accept because of the time factor. When you look at the concept of time with respect to our personal goals, patience and trust are key elements. When I started my training business in 1990, I set goals for myself and my business. One of my goals was to test market the High Performance Training Courses, and expand and sell sponsorships around the country within two years. I'm writing this in 1994, and I have yet to sell my first sponsorship. That doesn't mean that I won't reach this goal, it simply means that I need to be patient with the universe and trust that I have done the right things to achieve the goal. Sometimes our time factor and the time factor of the universe are quite different. If you look at what you have accomplished in your life and compare it to what has been accomplished over the past thirty years, and what will be accomplished in the future, your accomplishments are not much more than a nanosecond of time in the whole scope of things. So, keep the time factor in your memory bank and don't be too hard on yourself when you don't meet a particular deadline you've set.

LAW TWO. THE LAW OF NON-RESISTANCE tells us that resistance consumes our energy and slows us down. In the martial arts, the participants know that when they get pushed, it is best to refrain from pushing back. When you are pushed and go with the movement, you catch your opponent off guard and you have control. When you push back it takes more energy and you can lose control.

Practicing non-resistance is very important to us. To understand this, all you have to do is think like a goose. When you see a flock of geese heading south for the winter, notice that they are flying in a V formation. Science has discovered that, as each bird flaps its wings, it creates an uplift for the bird behind it. When geese fly in formation, they are using non-resistance, adding at least seventy-one percent greater flying range than if each flew individually. Whenever a goose falls out of formation, it begins to instantly feel the drag of resistance of going alone, and immediately gets back into the V formation to gain momentum. As High Performers we avoid resistance because whatever we resist persists. A dieter who resists certain foods experiences greater urges for those foods. The husband who resists showing affection to his wife makes her need that affection even more. Consequently she clings or complains, pushing the husband even further away.

I learned a great lesson about non-resistance in my business. I was going through great difficulty with cash flow. There never seemed to be quite enough. The less money I was bringing into my company, the harder I tried pushing my sales people to increase sales. The more I pushed, the more the sales people pushed our clients. When a salesperson needs to make a sale, she typically forgets the needs of the customer. Money becomes the entire focus. This creates blockages, making the customers defensive. Believe me, when customers are defensive, they won't buy much from you. When you stop resisting the natural flow of plenty in the universe, you will automatically bring plenty to you.

LAW THREE. THE LAW OF ADAPTATION tells us that when we adapt to our environment, we will survive and thrive. After living in Colorado for five years, I finally made it to the Continental Divide. The trip was truly amazing for me as I overlooked the magnificence of the scenery. As we climbed over fourteen thousand feet above sea level, I became tired, and my head hurt. The lack of oxygen at this altitude was affecting me. I found if I moved slower I felt better. This is adaptation. My body had to adapt to the surroundings. I also noticed that there were no trees. We were above timber line at that altitude. Because of the atmosphere, trees could not grow. The few bushes that did exist on the top of this mountain were bent and crooked from the harsh winds and heavy snowfall. Again, this is adaptation. In order for these bushes to exist, they had to adapt to the natural surroundings, no matter how difficult they were.

When I first went to work at Honeywell, I was in the shipping and receiving department. I wore jeans to work every day, and didn't give much thought to career advancement. After a couple of years, I was ready to move my career forward. I began applying for positions in production and inventory control. I was turned down every time. It didn't take me long to figure out that I didn't fit in to that environment. Everyone in production control wore suits and looked very professional. I invested in some new clothes and matched the new environment I wanted to work in. I found opportunities to assist the people in the department. I helped every chance I got. I spent time with them. It wasn't long until another position opened up for which I applied. I was a shoe-in. I had finally adapted to my environment. I learned as much as I could, as quickly as possible. Then I started to make changes. As High Performers, we must adapt to our environment in order to attain success. When we adapt, then and only then, can we make a difference and create positive change.

ATTRACTION FACTOR

After you understand the three natural laws, you'll find the attraction factor working for you. Whatever is happening to you is a result of the attraction factor. The attraction factor is your internal system which creates your reality from your beliefs. This system serves as a guide for your energy. Directing your positive or negative energy into the one which is the most dominant. For instance, perhaps you are working on your goals diligently and still not attaining them. This means your belief system is sending negative energy through your attraction system creating the reality that you should not attain those goals.

To attract or create the result that you want; you must change your belief system. This will send positive energy through your attraction system allowing your desired results to come to you. Use the "I Am's" to assist you in recreating your belief system so the attraction factor works in your favor.

GOING TO EXTREMES

As we seek personal balance in our lives we must strive for not too much and not too little. Just as our bodies must have a certain balance of nutrients and exercise to be healthy and energetic, so our minds must have the correct balance of knowledge and emotion. Our spiritual self must have enlightenment and growth. It's important to understand that going to extremes is not going to help you achieve personal balance. There are those people who exercise until they drop. The people who eat so little they develop anorexia. They want perfection. You've also watched the smoker who quits smoking and then becomes the non-smoker from HELL. I had a good friend who went through this transformation. She quit smoking after twenty years. Every time we went to a restaurant she would make a scene over people smoking. She was rude to smokers. She did this, under the guise of personal balance. Unfortunately, when she quit smoking to make herself healthier, she made the rest of us sick! I think W. Somerset Maughm said it all when he said, "It's a funny little thing about life. If you refuse to accept anything but the best, you very often get it."

PERSONAL BALANCE TRIAD

As High Performers it is important for us to understand the connection between our bodies, our minds and our emotions. Many people I meet think of each of these parts as operating completely separate from each other. It is vital to our success that we understand the important connection between our body, mind and spirit. Remember the last time you had a cold? Your body felt miserable, all tired and achey. At the same time, your mind was not as alert as it is typically.

Emotionally you were probably somewhat depressed.

You can also recall a day when you physically felt fantastic your mind was sharp, and you felt good about your existence. When you have a day like this, you can accomplish more, enjoy life to its fullest and relate better to everyone around you. This is exactly where we want to be as often as possible. Just think of it—a constant level of high performance! We're not striving for peak performance here, because where there are peaks, there are valleys. And I'm not saying that you'll always feel like you are on top of the world. But when you develop personal balance, you'll be able to jump from peak to peak instead, of falling down into those valleys. Even if you do fall into a slump, as a High Performer you are hardier and you'll bounce back quicker.

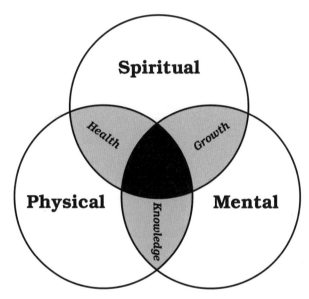

Diagram of personal balance - body, mind and spirit.

Every day ask yourself, "How can I enhance the center of the three circles?"

UNDERSTANDING THE TRIAD

1. MENTAL—GROWTH

The first area is mental. The 90s have been called the decade of the mind. As we move into the twenty-first century we must learn to use our whole brain and focus on increasing our mind capacity. Our mind controls what we think, feel, and do. It is imperative that we understand everything that we enter into our mind computer, so it allows us to operate at our fullest potential. As Wayne Dyer says, "You truly are what you think about all day long."

When dealing with your mind computer, it's important to program it with knowledge and information that will move you forward to success. It is essential to build each of the following aspects in your life so you can attain balance.

Confidence. Building your self-confidence by understanding your natural abilities and telling yourself that you are capable and competent is paramount to developing personal balance. Accepting yourself as the whole and perfect person that you are is the first step in attaining personal balance. This is why self-esteem is the first power in the success model.

Knowledge. With knowledge comes wisdom. Wisdom will allow you to understand personal balance and the whole concept of success. Knowledge is power. As you develop your wisdom, you develop your power. To develop your knowledge it's important to read, take classes and seminars, and join social and service groups to gain the wisdom of others. (Order the audio version of this book, called *The High Performance Success System* by calling 800-383-6919.)

Humor To gain and maintain balance it's imperative that you develop your sense of humor. Because of our impatience with the natural laws, it's even more important to maintain a good sense of humor. When you become over-anxious or set unrealistic goals for yourself, remember to keep things in perspective. Learn to laugh at the little things. Make a tense situation lighter with humor and balance comes easily.

As you're nurturing your mental state, remember that everything happens for a reason. This simple understanding will help you accept the natural laws and develop personal balance.

TIPS FOR MENTAL PROSPERITY

- **Use meditation techniques to get in touch with your inner self.**

- **Let go of past failures, problems and negatives.**

- **Be patient with yourself—accept who you are right now.**

- **Trust your intuition and respond to it with joy.**

- Go with the flow—don't resist change, become it.

- Every day spend time widening, opening, and changing your perspective on challenges and life in general.

- Become mindful, be aware of yourself and everything around you.

- Read, listen and learn from everyone.

- Every day look at one way to make yourself better, nicer, smarter, and more balanced.

2. PHYSICAL—HEALTH

You know how important it is to maintain a strong healthy body in order to be a High Performer. I'm not going to lecture you on maintaining an exercise ritual or becoming a health food fanatic. What I am going to tell you about is gaining balance—not too much and not too little. My mother was an amazing woman. Unfortunately, she died when she was only forty-five years old. Why? Because she didn't have balance. In 1972 we didn't know as much about nutrition as we now do, and if we had, my mom might be alive today. She was raised during the depression in a very poor family. Mom spent several years in an orphanage with several of her brothers and sisters because her mother couldn't afford to care for them. All during her life, because of her circumstances, she ate fried, fatty foods, and rarely had fiber in her diet. She gained a lot of weight and spent most of her adult life weighing over three hundred pounds. She died of colon cancer in 1972. I remember her telling me that too much of anything would cause cancer. I believe she was right.

It is critical to eat a healthy diet to maintain high performance. I'm not talking about extremes. I simply mean that you must eat a balanced diet. Avoid sugar, caffeine, alcohol, nicotine, salt, smog, and pesticides that cause physical problems. These increase stress which keep you from being a high performance person. There are more nutrition books out now than any of us could ever read, so there is no excuse for continuing to survive on junk foods.

As far as exercise, I say, "Work hard and play hard." Get involved in a sport that you enjoy. Maybe hiking, or biking, or even swimming. Don't place radical requirements on yourself because this will cause you to avoid exercise. The important thing to remember is that you can't sit on the couch flipping TV channels and expect to be in shape. Get out and walk. Park your car further from your destination and walk. Take the steps instead of the elevator. Take a physical vacation, like caving or mountain biking. Go dancing! When you get involved with life, exercise is fun.

The other physical area that is critical to all High Performers is rest. I know many people who suffer from lack of sleep. They're not as effective as they could be because their minds are dulled and their bodies are sluggish. In order to have balance you must get exercise and rest.

TIPS FOR PHYSICAL PROSPERITY

- **Treat your body as you do your best friend or your child—**

    Nurture it

    Love it unconditionally

    Want what's best for it

    Accept it as is

    Don't abuse it

    Do your best for it

    Make it a top priority

    Give it what it needs to be its best

- **Have fun in your favorite sport and exercise will be easy.**

- **Avoid extremes.**

- **Listen to your body, it will tell you what it needs.**

- **Protect it from hazards: too much sun, drugs, too much alcohol, unsafe sex or physical abuse.**

- **Become the manager of your physical department and organize a plan for making it the best run department in your whole organization.**

3. SPIRITUAL—KNOWLEDGE

Finally, the spiritual area. Remember that your spiritual being is a very important part of your life. When you ignore it, you are out of balance. When I speak of the spiritual state, I am referring to your consciousness, and your emotions or feelings. We have an obligation in our world to not only care for ourselves and our families, but to reach out to all humanity. My dear friend, Marina Raye, who co-founded the High Performance Training, has written about a magical journey of self-discovery. She talks about our higher purpose and truly understanding our spiritual being. I gained much from her wisdom and teachings. She helped me understand much about our emotional state of being. Marina teaches that fear begets fear. The more we are afraid, the more fear enters our mind. Anger holds us back, and resentment keeps us from reaching our potential. She also teaches that any strength taken to extremes is a weakness. We must be aware of our emotional states in order to have balance.

It is also important to understand that we are all part of a much larger picture. As Dr. Wayne Dyer states, we are all connected to all of humanity. It is critical as a High Performer that we believe and nurture this connection through acceptance. When we accept our connection to the universe, our whole life becomes easier and more fruitful.

I have found it interesting that my body will tell me when I am out of balance. When I have not eaten the right type of foods, I gain weight or have heartburn. When I don't get enough exercise or rest, my muscles become weak and my back aches. When I spend all my time working, I start to feel lonely and disconnected from my family and everyone else around me. It doesn't take a lot of effort for me to start eating the right balance of foods and take a walk or even reach out to my husband and kids. I just have to do it! When you develop personal balance, you are naturally in control of your world. Remember, your results come in direct proportion to the effort that you put forth.

TIPS FOR SPIRITUAL PROSPERITY

- **Accept your spiritual self.**

- **Write out your spiritual goals.**

- **Be open to new spiritual ideas.**

- **Share your spiritual beliefs with others who share those beliefs.**

- **Make your consciousness a priority to maintain and develop.**

- **Feel your emotions and learn what they represent.**

- **Seek out guidance to help you develop your spiritual self.**

- **Think in global terms: community v self; world v. country, and universe v. galaxy**

- **Look at all beliefs and value the diversity.**

EXERCISE

Here's an exercise to help you understand the concept of personal balance. You've probably heard the term "centering." This is an exercise in centering yourself. With a partner, stand about twelve inches apart. Have your partner place their index finger on the middle of your breast bone. Have him push. You'll probably fall backward until you catch yourself.

Now, close your eyes and imagine all of your strength, all of your essence, in a small ball in the middle of your body. This ball should be mentally placed about one inch above your naval. Feel the strength and feel the power. Now, have your partner do the same pushing technique as before. This time you cannot be budged because you are centered or balanced.

EXERCISE

Write out three things you can do in each of these areas to help you develop more balance in yourself and your life:

Mental   _____

_____

_____

Spiritual   _____

_____

_____

Volitional
(your will)

_____

_____

_____

Emotional:

_____

_____

_____

Physical:

_____

_____

_____

Social:

_____

_____

_____

Once you have written these out, fill out a gold action card (These cards can be ordered by calling 800 383-6919) or an index card and keep it with you so you will remember to work on these items each day.

To sum up the importance of personal balance, I want to share a story.

> There was a woman who found a cocoon on the
> branch of a tree outside her home. She was amazed
> after examining the cocoon that it was an emperor
> moth. It was named this because of its five-inch wing
> span and beautiful magenta color. She was so excited
> she could hardly wait for the cocoon to transform into
> a moth. One day as she passed the cocoon, she
> heard a noise and saw that the cocoon was moving
> on the branch of the tree. She knew it was time for
> the moth to emerge from the cocoon. She looked close-
> ly and saw a tiny hole on the top of the cocoon.
> Trying as hard as it could the moth couldn't make it
> through the tiny hole. Every day she returned to
> watch the cocoon shake and rattle on the branch.
> And on the fourth day she felt so sorry for the moth
> that she got a pin and made the hole a little larger so

the moth could break through. And she was right; on its next attempt, the moth started pulling itself through the hole. She watched as the magnificent moth emerged from the cocoon. Then she was saddened as the moth fell to the ground and died. She realized that it was intended for the moth to go through that tiny hole so that its wings would be elongated and strengthened for its first solo flight.

We are all like that moth. We are created to go through those tiny holes in life to strengthen us and enable us to reach our potential in a natural progression, with adaptability and non-resistance. You can be like the man in the opening story who gained and lost four fortunes. Or you can develop personal balance. When you do, high performance success is swift and immediate.

ACTION PAGE

The great aim of education is not knowledge, but ACTION.
-Herbert Spencer

ACTION STEPS
To High Performance

The major benefit I gained from this chapter was:

_____

_____

_____

_____

Based on this benefit, my High Performance Action Plan is:

_____

_____

_____

_____

Why is this action plan important to me?

_____

_____

_____

_____

The Motivation

"Motivation is described as that which moves you forward. The powers in this section are motivating forces. Here is where you fuel your desire for which you are inclined."

Chapter 10

Creativity: The Whole Brain Adventure

The creative mind plays with the objects it loves.
Carl Jung

When I ask groups, "What is creativity?" I typically hear these responses: "free thinking," "imagination," "unique," "anything goes," "fun," "collision of two unrelated ideas," "exploring," "the road less traveled," "wild," "crazy," "inventive," "right brain," "art," "spontaneous," and "childlike." These are really good responses and describe creativity quite well. After we have discussed creativity, I'll get responses like "risk taking," "flexibility," "genius," "productivity," "ingenuity," and "teaming imagination." These concepts take creativity a little further into whole brain thinking.

I'll tell you what I think creativity is, I think it is POWER. I think creativity unleashes our power to solve problems, start businesses, develop new products, create ideas for sales, make resolutions, and increase effectiveness. Every skill in the High Performance Success System is magnified by creativity. Everything you do in life is enhanced by being more creative. Power number seven is Creativity: the Whole Brain Adventure.

I have always nurtured my creative side, but when I really became involved in my career, it seemed to dwindle. I began to doubt my intuition and was reluctant to take risks. My approach to work seemed to be what was rewarded in the corporate environment. Slowly I began to notice a change in management styles. As TQM programs were implemented and customer service programs were taking hold, I could see a definite shift in the thinking in business. Suddenly, I was rewarded for speaking my mind and stepping outside normal boundaries. I remember the first time my supervisor asked me what I thought we should do about a program that was off schedule and over budget. I nearly fell off my chair! Of course I knew the program better than anyone and I knew how to resolve several of the issues, but I had never been asked to share my opinion. I knew then that there was definitely something going on in the business environment that was bigger than all of us.

There is definitely a revolution occurring within business—a revolution to break away from old style thinking and into the right mode. A revolution moving away from treating employees like children, instead allowing them to do the jobs they were hired to do. I was EXCITED! Finally I was a real human being who was important to this organization. But then, I was shot down. My boss started off well, but stifled my thought process and my courage by stating the changes I suggested couldn't be done, and that I must be crazy to even recommend them! So much for employee empowerment.

From this example you can see how we are all knocked down and stuffed into our business roles. Our creativity is stifled daily by managers who are still living in a business world which no longer exists. This is why it is critical for each of us to revolutionize ourselves, thinking of ourselves as self-employed. Think of new ways to approach your boss. Give her three solutions and point out the benefits to each. If it doesn't work the first time, try again, and again, and again. Creativity is risk-taking, and risk-taking is power. When you have power you can change the entire course of any business.

CREATIVITY FROM HIGH PERFORMERS

Several graduates of my training are business owners. Here's how some of them have opened up their own creativity to inspire their employees to a higher team spirit.

The owner of a small mortgage loan company with six employees laid down a challenge. She asked each employee where they would like to go for their dream vacation. Most said Hawaii, and the others agreed that would be a great vacation. Then the boss asked how many more closings each could make during a month. They shared a number and the boss did some calculations. She said if they closed a certain number of loans each month, she would pay for all of them to take a one-week cruise around the Hawaiian islands. They achieved the goal, made the trip, and continue to strive together as a focused team!

Another graduate wanted to increase her cosmetic sales. It was Christmas time, a time when sales for her business were typically slow. She dressed like an elf and carried a basket of samples. She walked through every store downtown handing out samples. She acquired several new clients with this risky venture.

Another participant wanted a job with another of our clients. We had introduced her, recommended her, the rest was up to her. She interviewed and found she was lacking in important computer skills. She called several times, reinforcing her enthusiasm for the position, but didn't get an answer. Finally she wrote a poem to the potential employer. When the employer received the poem she called her saying that anyone with that much initiative would benefit her company, and hired her.

There are lots of ways to use your creativity. Use your creativity to solve problems at work or to generate ideas to help you raise funds for a charity. Use creativity to get your child to pick up his room or your spouse to mow the lawn.

TRUSTING YOUR INTUITION

Creativity is using your ingenuity. Don't judge your ideas. Simply trust that your hunch is right. That's your intuition. I've lived my life using my intuition. I know the one person in the world I can trust is me. Ask yourself these questions:

"How can I solve this problem?" "What should I do to change this situation?" "Is this the right way to handle this issue?" And then—listen.

The more you trust your intuition, the more you will listen to it. Thomas Edison would take naps at any time of day in order to listen to his intuition. Have you ever been sitting in a meeting and suddenly a little voice or picture comes to you? All of a sudden it's crystal clear how to solve your problem. Learn to stop judging your hunches. Don't let your left brain kick in and act like the manager I described earlier, stifling some of your greatest ideas.

When you get hunches, write them down immediately. I can't tell you how many times I've gotten an idea, only to forget it or not act on it. This happened to me when my eighteen-year-old son was a baby. One day I was changing his diaper. After the diaper leaked all over my rug, I got an idea that I should create a disposable diaper with elastic around the legs so it couldn't leak. This was in 1975. Just a short time after that a diaper company came out with that diaper. When you get hunches, write them down and act on them. It might be the BIG idea you've been waiting for!

TIPS FOR TRUSTING YOUR INTUITION

- Start small. Trust a little hunch and when it works out you'll feel confident to take bigger risks.

- Talk to others who work on intuition. Ask them how they know when they should trust or not trust.

- Learn to stop evaluating every hunch. Logic interferes with creative thinking. When you get a hunch, act on it quickly so there is no time to evaluate.

- Take a deep breath and go with the feeling.

- Prepare yourself for some errors. Knowing in advance that every hunch may not work out gives you the ability to fail occasionally. Here's where you can evaluate. Look at the failure and evaluate what was wrong.

- Look at danger as opportunity. In China there is no word for crisis. It is symbolized by two characters meaning danger/opportunity.

- Practice being intuitive. At first you can see if the hunch works out without acting on it.

- Keep track of successes from your intuition. We have a tendency to discount our ideas, especially when they are merely hunches.

MIND MAPPING®

I gained a valuable skill that I want to share with you which will enhance your creativity immediately. It's called Mind Mapping® or, as I like to call it, idea mapping. Tony Buzan has written about Mind Mapping® in a book called, *Use Both Sides of Your Brain.* Before beginning an idea map, be sure to "switch-on" the whole brain by doing the cross crawl, or another exercise from educational kinesiology. If you have ever done any brainstorming, you'll understand Mind Mapping® easily.

To understand a Mind Map® you must realize what it is. Mind Mapping® was originated in 1970 by Tony Buzan. A Mind Map® is a technique using pictures to harness the power of your brain. Harnessing your full range of brain skills: words, images, numbers, logic, rhythm, colors and spacial awareness. All of this in one manner—The Mind Map®.

Similar to a road map or a blueprint, the idea map will:

- assist you in problem solving

- help you develop lots of new and interesting ideas

- be more efficient than brainstorming

There are laws or rules for Mind Mapping® which will help you in using this technique to its fullest extent. Here they are:

1. **Start in the center with a picture of the topic or problem. (Use several bright colors.)**

2. **Use pictures and symbols throughout the map.**

3. **Use key words printed on lines radiating from the center.**

4. **Use single words or short phrases on each line.**

5. **Use lots of color throughout the map—your own design.**

6. **Create your own style of Mind Mapping®.**

7. **Do not judge your own ideas.**

8. **Use words or phrases which are related to the topic or totally unrelated.**

9. **Gets lots of people involved for a highly creative Mind Map®.**

10. **Evaluate the map when you are finished.**

It doesn't take long to generate several great ideas. At our office, when we are stumped over a problem or need a new idea, we bring in some neighbors from surrounding businesses and create an idea map. In five minutes we fill up two marker boards with good information. Later we can evaluate and implement the ideas.

To evaluate the ideas, look over the list, determining if any of the ideas are easily linked together. Draw a line connnecting these ideas. Use your whole brain to check the feasibility and practicality of your items. Watch for items that really stand out; maybe they are unique or even a simple idea you've been overlooking. If a new theme evolves, just create another MIND MAP® around that major point.

How can you use idea mapping? Here's how one of our graduates used MIND MAPPING® to solve a problem: The owner of a small tv station in southern Colorado found idea mapping to be his favorite tool. He wanted to take his staff to New Orleans when the Denver Broncos were in the Super Bowl, but they didn't have the funds for such an expensive trip. After learning this technique, he got his staff together and they created an idea map using the unrelated style. Here's an illustration of what happened:

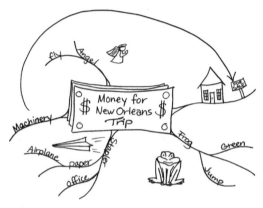

He said if they hadn't used idea mapping, they might not have thought of selling the equipment.

Another client used idea mapping in her architecture firm. She works with churches renovating or building new churches. She says the whole congregation gets involved in the planning. Idea mapping was perfect for this situation. She got as many people from the church together as possible, and she introduced idea mapping to decide the types of rooms they wanted, and the items they couldn't live without. She had an entire wall filled with an idea map in her office. She involved everyone.

Another way to use idea mapping is to use it to take notes in school. Several graduates who are students in high school or college have told us how they have used idea mapping for note taking. It is simpler and enables them to remember the information easier. I use idea mapping to create an outline for talks I give to groups. I can use the colorful idea map as my visual aid. People enjoy seeing it. My outline is right in front of me so I never forget any information I want to share with my audience. Another graduate told me she uses idea mapping to help clients at her radio station to come up with new ideas to use for advertising their products. Another client who works for state government was assigned a new project about which he knew nothing. He didn't want to look like he was ignorant, so he started an idea map. He took it to each person he knew was familiar with the project and asked them to add to the idea map so he would be sure not to leave anything out. He saved his idea map and used it in his final presentation to project members. Here's an idea map I use for a presentation I give on whole brain creativity:

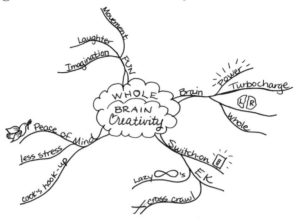

SWITCHING-ON EXERCISES

Prior to using the idea mapping technique, you can use more exercises from EK to enhance your creativity. Here's how:

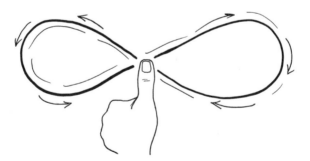

The Lazy 8's

Use this exercise when you are writing. Extend your hand straight out in front of you with your fist closed and your thumb pointing up. Starting in an upward stroke to the left, draw an "8" lying on its side. As you do this, follow your thumb with your eyes. Only your arm and eyes should be moving. Your eyes and arm are crossing the mid-line. Switch hands and do the same thing with the other arm. Then clasp your hands together and draw the Lazy 8 with both hands.

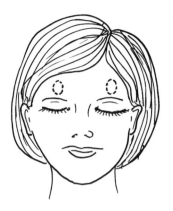

Brain Buttons

This is a great technique for relaxing and clearing the mind. Sit in a relaxed, upright manner. Place your index fingers on your forehead just above each eye where there is a slight indentation. Press firm, not hard. Close your eyes and take a few deep breaths.

Switching on the whole brain will unleash your creativity and increase your personal power.

TURBOCHARGE YOUR CREATIVITY

Turbocharge your creativity by doing things differently. We have a tendency to let ourselves fall into patterns. These patterns keep us from using more of our brain and our potential. Here are several ideas for turbocharging your creativity:

- **Take a new route to work.**

- **Put your mascara on beginning with the opposite eye you usually begin with.**

- **Start shaving on the opposite side or a different part of your face each morning.**

- **If you usually put on sock, sock, shoe, shoe— change and put on sock, shoe, sock, shoe.**

- **Use your non-dominant hand as much as possible. You probably won't want to use a fork or razor for this one, but you can doodle, scratch, or drink with your non-dominant hand.**

- **Spend a weekend using only your non-dominant hand and you'll be amazed how much more creative you'll be.**

- **Do things just ten percent differently.**

- **Don't do the same things; try something new, break your typical patterns.**

- **Always ask questions, no matter how trivial.**
- **Always look for change in everything.**
- **Wing it!**
- **Expand on a thought.**
- **Draw a picture of the problem.**
- **Put your problem into a different environment.**
- **Think like a child.**
- **Ask yourself a question and then listen for the answer.**
- **Stand on top of the problem for a different perspective.**
- **Ask a stranger for input to your problem.**
- **Always find more than one right answer to every problem.**
- **Become MacGuyver and solve your problem.**
- **Let your mind wander—daydream.**

Do something outrageous, like starting a meeting with everyone in the room standing up while half the people moo like cows, and the other half gobble like turkeys. Keep this up for a full thirty seconds. We use animal sounds when teach our children about animals, but we tend to be embarrassed to make animal noises with other adults. Break free from your inhibitions and your creativity will soar.

SENSORY AWARENESS

Becoming more aware of, and using all your senses will also enhance your creativity. I'm going to take you through an exercise in creative muscle flexing that will require you to close your eyes and relax. You may want to save this exercise for when you will not be interrupted. Use the workbook to guide you, and a partner, through this exercise. As you are going through this exercise, realize that many people have difficulty visualizing, but don't worry. Just get a feel for the picture and with practice the picture will come. You will be experiencing scenes through all of your senses.

Close your eyes. Take a couple of deep breaths.

Simply relax and clear your mind. Visualize a sunset over the mountains. Make it a vivid scene. Notice the bright colors and see animals carefully moving about. Next, see your front door—yes, the door on the front of your home. What color is it? Does it have glass or is it solid wood? How many locks are on this door? Is there a door knocker? Let's move on to the next scene. Visualize your dream home. What style is it—a two-story or a ranch? What color is it? How many windows are there? Get a clear picture of your dream home.

Now we are switching from seeing to hearing. Hear the sound of a friend laughing. How does it sound? Loud or soft? Maybe it's a belly laugh. Now, hear the sound of thunder as it cracks, and rain as it beats down on a tin roof. Hear the sound as the thunder clears and the rain stops and becomes a slow drop here and there. Hear the sound of a motor racing. Hear the engine rev up and slow down. Hear how it sounds as it pulls away.

Next let's feel things. Feel your feet running through wet grass. Feel the feeling of diving into ice cold water. Feel a cat rubbing against your bare leg. How do these things feel? Uncomfortable, creepy, or just bad?

Now let's smell things. Smell burning toast in your kitchen. Smell fish frying. Smell freshly cut grass early in the summer. How are these smells? Do they conjure up pictures in your mind?

Now you will be tasting things. Taste a freshly cut lemon as you squeeze it into your mouth. Are you unpuckered yet? Taste your mouth in the morning as you put your toothbrush filled with toothpaste against your teeth and start to brush. Let's get hungry. Taste freshly cut pineapple. Taste how sweet and tart it is.

Finally, you will be experiencing emotions. Experience the emotion of extreme happiness. You know, some time when you did something extremely well. Feel how good it is. Feel the emotion of saying goodbye to a dear friend. How does this feel? Is it sad? Is it exciting? Feel the emotion of falling in love. How do you feel? Is it a wonderful feeling or is it a peaceful feeling? Now that you have experienced using all of your senses, relax and when you are ready you can open your eyes.

Going through this type of exercise is a very helpful tool in creativity awareness. We are all very creative, we just don't realize it. Becoming aware of pictures, smells, tastes, feelings and emotions helps us become more aware of everything around us, helping us become more creative. We become open to new ideas and allow them to stir up even more ideas.

CREATIVITY BOOSTERS

By yourself or with your staff, have a creativity meeting. Spend at least one hour doing any or all of the following:

1. **Create a new company logo using crayons from a child's point of view.**

2. **Cut out several cartoons from magazines or newspapers and leave off the captions. Create new captions from song titles.**

3. **Tell a pick-it-up-from-here story. You start by saying, Mary is the CEO for a large space needle company. Her production manager just reported that 500 space needles are being returned because they bend in half when they hit an altitude of 30,000 feet. (Point to someone to "pick it up from there," taking over the imaginary story. Continue until everyone has participated.)**

4. **List every advantage you or your group can think of for having an eye in your index finger. (Use an idea map for fun.)**

5. **Think of at least five improvements for a snow shovel.**

6. **Come up with ten new uses for the common brick.**

7. **List as many ways as possible to ensure you provide the world's worst customer service.**

8. **Create the house of the future—Year 2060.**

9. **Determine six new ways to invite people to a party.**

10. **Come up with at least five good reasons to receive junk mail.**

UNLEASH YOUR THINKING

Get out of your box thinking. Connect these nine dots with four straight lines without raising your pencil from the paper or crossing over lines:

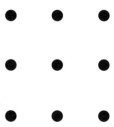

Now do the same thing, only with one line:

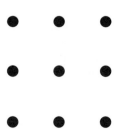

Answers are in the appendix. People tend to think in terms of lines and linear patterns. Be creative and break out of your box thinking.

BRAIN AEROBICS

To become more creative it's helpful to challenge your mind. Play word games that force you to think in a different way. Here are two mind games. They represent familiar phrases, simply decipher the other meaning of the sets of words: (Answers are in Appendix A.)

1 i n w a i t	2 ho ho + ho	3 LOVE SIGHT SIGHT SIGHT	4 **WR*it* ING**
5 G R E N A I S N O	6 N O S^E	7 **PETS A**	8 S O L DANUBE
9 Symphon	10 **encounters encounters encounters**	11 3. O 2. U 1. T	12 1 3 5 7 9 11 vs. U
13 **eyebrows**	14 r o rail d	15 **T RN**	16 budget ∧

1 PERSON PERSONS PERSONS PERSONS	**2** insult + injury	**3** EVARELTO	**4** (S T E A K)^3
5 NO WAYS IT WAYS	**6** ALL world	**7** 1 3 5 7 9 **WHELMING**	**8** **CCCCCCC**
9 **gettingitall**	**10** **alai**	**11** **CUS TOM**	**12** **MAUD**
13 T T +T — 3T	**14** **RASINGINGIN**	**15** FAIRY WOLF DUCKLING	**16** **24 Hours**

(Reprinted from the book, *Still More Games Trainers Play*, John W. Newstrom, Edward E. Scannell, 1991. Used with permission of the publisher, McGraw-Hill.)

Success comes in many ways and we all need to be watching for it. When we use more of our brain, paying closer attention to our intuition, we're more apt to grab hold of success instead of letting it slip by. I'd like to end this chapter with this final story:

> *There was a little girl who passed by a sculptor's studio each day. She noticed that he was beginning work on a large, beautiful slab of marble. She came by each day for several weeks and watched curiously as the sculptor worked his magic on the marble. Finally, she noticed the head of a magnificent lion appear under the sculptor's masterful hands. She quickly went inside the studio and asked, "Did you know that was in there all the time?"*

We all have a very creative person buried inside of us. Switch on your whole brain and dig out your creative person.

ACTION PAGE

The great aim of education is not knowledge, but ACTION.
-Herbert Spencer

ACTION STEPS
To High Performance

The major benefit I gained from this chapter was:

_____

_____

_____

_____

Based on this benefit, my High Performance Action Plan is:

_____

_____

_____

_____

Why is this action plan important to me?

_____

_____

_____

_____

Chapter 11

Goal Setting: The Ten Realms of Outcome Planning

What would you do if you knew you could not fail?
Robert Schuller

D o you have everything you want in life? If you do, then skip this chapter. If not, continue reading and hold onto your seats because this is where things start to happen.

About fifty percent of the participants in my seminars don't have goals. The other fifty percent don't have clear, written goals. Why don't more people plan their future? Because it takes work. Yes, it takes time and effort to establish what you want and how to get it. Planning our outcomes is critical to achieving High Performance. This is why we've developed a special format for planning your outcomes. The eighth power in the success model is Goal Setting: The 10 Realms of Outcome Planning. When you go through this process you will get results very quickly!

WHAT IS OUTCOME PLANNING?

Why do I refer to goal setting as outcome planning? After giving many presentations on goals in which I ask my audiences how many people have goals and reach all those goals, it became apparent that people tend to be intimidated by the word GOAL. It almost becomes overwhelming for many people. Being the master reframer that I am, I reframed the term "goal setting" to "outcome planning" because we always have an outcome. When we begin as if we are already there, it's exhilarating, rather than intimidating.

WHY IS OUTCOME PLANNING IMPORTANT?

Before I talk about the ten realms, let's understand why goal setting, or outcome planning, is so important. I spent several years working as a product planner for a manufacturer of computer chips. During this time I developed my understanding of the absolute necessity of outcome planning. When an order was received from a customer, it was the beginning of the outcome planning process. The order was sent through marketing to a product planner. The product planner, my job, would oversee the project from introduction into the production line to shipping the product to the customer. I would meet with every department involved on the project. This meeting would serve as a kickoff to let all the players know who was involved and to allow me to gather pertinent information about the product itself. I would gather such information as the following:

- **How many parts does the customer want?**

- **When does the customer want the parts?**

- **What are the customer's specifications?**

- **How is the part to be built?**

- **Is this a standard part or a new part?**

- **Do we have the raw materials on hand?**

- **and so on. . .**

After gathering all the information, I could begin developing the plan. I always started with the customer's required quantity and then, using the yield information from engineering, I went back through the entire process, until I had the necessary parts to be started into the line. After the parts were started into the line, I checked them daily, or as needed, to ensure we were on schedule. Meetings were held with the entire team for status reports on the project at regular intervals. Sometimes problems would occur and create challenges for the project team, like not having enough raw materials or low yields requiring more parts be started into the beginning of the production line, or even the customer changing their requirements. Every day I checked the product to make sure it was moving on schedule. When the prod-

160

uct shipped to the customer, there was always a celebration—sometimes big and sometimes small, but you can be guaranteed that it felt great. The next day, I moved on to the next project feeling good and ready to go.

Why is outcome planning so important? Based on the information I have just shared with you, there are five very good reasons why it is important:

1. Outcome planning gives you a final destination.

2. Outcome planning gives you clear direction.

3. Outcome planning helps you stay on track.

4. Outcome planning will help you achieve more.

5. Outcome planning builds enthusiasm into your life.

Why are these five items true? Let's look back at the information about the production planner and it'll be easy to see why. When you have a desire to accomplish something, or an idea to make something happen, that's the beginning of the goal setting process. Just like the planner, you take this idea, or desire, to positive friends and relatives who support you and check the feasibility. Many people let the process stop even before they talk to anyone about it. After getting input from others, you simply lay out your plan.

● **What is my final vision?**

● **When do I want to achieve it?**

● **What do I need to do to make it happen?**

● **Do I have the personal strengths and resources to make it happen?**

● **Who can help me achieve this outcome?**

Then every day you watch your plan. You meet with people when necessary who can help you continue moving toward your outcome. Never, never, never stray from your final vision. Always remain focused on your end desire. Sometimes you'll have specifications or yields that change in your life, That's fine—you simply amend your plan and stay on track. When you have achieved your outcome, celebrate and renew your enthusiasm for your next planned outcome.

THE SMART METHOD

Goal setting is important, and it is important to be SMART when planning your outcomes. Here's what I mean by being **SMART**. The **S** in this acronym stands for being **specific**. Whenever you plan an outcome it must be stated in terms that are specific and understandable. Instead of saying, "I want to increase my sales," say, "I want to increase my sales by twenty percent by the end of this month." You can't plan something that is vague.

The **M** stands for **measurable.** Your goals must be in a form that can be measured: "I want to increase my sales every week by five percent." You can measure weekly to see how you are doing against your goals. The **A** stands for **action-oriented.** When you plan an outcome, it's important to build in steps that will move you forward immediately. Goals are never achieved by lack of action. Breaking the big goal into smaller pieces make it easier to achieve.

The **R** stands for **realistic.** Is your goal something that you can achieve? Remember, if you're forty-five years old and have never played football, it isn't likely that you are going to become an NFL super star in the next year or two. Make sure that your goals are realistic for you. And finally, the **T** stands for **true.** Are your goals true for you or are they really someone else's goals? Too many times we take on goals that someone else wants us to achieve and we drag our feet to make things happen. It's very important to use the SMART method—**Specific, Measurable, Action-oriented, Realistic and True**—when planning your outcomes.

CORE DESIRE

Something else that I believe is very important in outcome planning is, understanding the concept of core desires. What is a core desire? A core desire represents the goal, or goals, that have the highest priority in your life at that moment. Take a moment and write down a goal that you have in each of the following areas: career, family, spiritual, financial, or physical. Rate these goals on a scale from one to one hundred, with one being the least important to you and one hundred being the most important to you. This will help you understand the concept of core desire. Use the information in your workbook for this exercise. Any of the goals that you rated below ninety on the scale are probably not very important to you. Any of the goals that you rated in the ninety to one hundred, range, you will most likely achieve and achieve quickly. You can still achieve the goals you rated low, but it will probably take longer to achieve them, if you ever do. Simply understand that in order for you to achieve your planned outcomes in the timeframe you desire, they must be rated accordingly on the scale. Any goal that is considered a core desire is the goal that you will work on with a passion, and it will happen.

I always had a passion for learning. When I was in grade school, I set a goal to graduate from college. No one in my family had ever graduated from college, and it was a true passion for me. I knew that I wanted to go into business management, and I dreamed of the day when I would run my own business. Unfortunately, in high school I got distracted and dropped out of school. However, since learning was a core desire for me, it wasn't long before I was back in night school and graduated from high school. Shortly after that, even though I was married and had a small child, I enrolled in college. Again, because of other responsibilities, I got distracted and it took me several years. However, since this was still a core desire for me, at the age of thirty-six, I graduated from college with a BSBA in Management and I went on from there to get my Masters. I'm still passionate about learning. We can get OFF PLAN and still attain our planned outcomes if it is truly a core desire. It doesn't matter how long the journey to the goal takes, if it's a core desire for you, you will reach it! Use the following diagram to determine your core desires.

1	50	100

Write a brief goal for each of the following areas. Then rate each, on the above scale, 1 being the least important to you, 100 being the most important this minute. Put these answers in the "as is" column. Then rate them according to where they should rate according to the information about core desires. Put this in the "should be" column.

SCORE

As Is   Should Be

1. **Family:**_____ _____ _____

2. **Career:**_____ _____ _____

3. **Spiritual:**_____ _____ _____

4. **Social:**_____ _____ _____

5. **Health/Physical**_____ _____ _____

6. **Education/Self Improvement**_____ _____ _____

7. **Other:**_____ _____ _____

8. **Other:**_____ _____ _____

CYCLE OF GOALS

When you determine your goals and start taking action there is a cycle that takes over as the following diagram shows:

VISUALIZATION AND IMAGERY

The most frequently given excuse I hear from clients is, "I don't have time to write down goals. It's just too much trouble." I was one of these people. I always had goals, but they were only written in my mind. Because of this I didn't always stick to a plan to keep me moving toward my goals. In the process that follows I will ask you to do much more than just write down your goals. I will help you involve many more of your senses and emotions. Visualization is one of the steps I'll take you through. This is a favorite of mine, since I'm a visual person.

I was watching a morning news show and heard a story about a football team in Animas, New Mexico, several years ago. The team, located at a school in the middle of a desert didn't have spectacular athletes, nor did they have the same athletes over several years. Yet they had won over forty-five straight football games. They had gained notice from the media who asked the coach how they had accomplished such a feat. The coach said he had the boys go into the library before every game and visualize every pass, every play, every touch down and finally winning the game. Then they went out on the field and did what they had visualized. That night was their final game of the season. A couple of weeks went by and I wondered how the team had done. I called Animas High School. I explained the situation to the lady who answered and I asked if the team had won their final game. I heard her voice drop as she answered, "No, we lost." She said that the team had gotten so much attention from the media that everyone began focusing on the negatives.

When you focus on your goals and visualize yourself achieving them, you are propelled forward. Visualizing and creating mental images and attaching symbolism to those images is very powerful in goal achieving. I use these methods all the time. I plan an outcome, write it down, and visualize having achieved the goal (getting emotionally involved in the scene). Then I create an image of my energy moving out into the universe and the goal coming back to me as if I am a magnet. You can create any image or symbol that works for you. Be creative!

THE TEN REALMS OF OUTCOME PLANNING

I'm going to share with you the Ten Realms of Outcome Planning. This is a very important process. Follow the instructions to gain the most. There is a space so you can write in this book. I will share a task with you and you should complete the information. This is critical to your success. After you have gone through this process, you'll be amazed at the things that start to happen for you. A married couple in my training went through this process separately, finding that they had different goals. When they went through this process together, they had similar goals. Now they are moving toward their goals together. Their businesses have increased and they're building a new home. They planned their outcomes in advance and success followed.

> Go to a quiet place where you will not be interrupted. You'll need a pen, lots of paper, and an open mind. Sit where you will be comfortable and can write easily. Go through the Lazy 8's exercise to switch on your whole brain. Now you're ready to begin.

> **Realm I.** Create a Christmas list of desired outcomes (remember to use the SMART method). For this realm, assume you have no limits. Take your time and write down everything you ever want to do, see, or accomplish. As Robert Schuller asks, "What would you do if you knew you could not fail?" Have you always dreamed of taking a trip around the world, or learning to fly an airplane? Make sure you list goals in every category of your life. Take your time and write down every last desired outcome you want to achieve.

Christmas list of outcomes you desire:

_____

_____

_____

_____

_____

_____

_____

_____

_____

_____

_____

_____

_____

_____

_____

Realm II. Didn't that feel good! Writing down your desires is a very powerful experience. Go back to your list, look it over, ranking the goals in order of importance to you. Again take your time, determining which of your desires is number 1, and number 2, and so forth.

Realm III. Was it difficult to narrow down the top two or three items? If so, that's okay, sometimes we have more than one core desire. Take your time and write a paragraph for each desired outcome, explaining why it's important for you to obtain it. Maybe it will fulfill a childhood dream, or would make your life better, or help society. Be specific and complete, don't miss any—just take your time.

Realm IV. Tired of writing yet? Stand up and stretch. Do the Cross Crawl. Looking over your list of outcomes, determine when each outcome will occur, the year, month and day. Again, take your time and be complete.

Realm V. Take your time and write a list of your personal strengths and resources which will help you in attaining your planned outcomes. Are you resourceful, or highly organized, or maybe you have good communication skills, or friends and family who can help, perhaps a financial resource you hadn't thought of before. Take your time and don't overlook anything.

_____

_____

_____

_____

_____

_____

_____

_____

_____

_____

_____

_____

_____

_____

_____

_____

_____

Realm VI. List five or six mentors who will give you advice to attain each outcome. These can be someone you know, or someone who has written a book, or someone you admire. Maybe Ben Franklin, Ross Perot, or even your dad, would share some words of wisdom with you. Just imagine and write down what advice they would give you.

_____

_____

_____

_____

_____

_____

_____

_____

_____

_____

_____

_____

Realm VII. Get comfortable. Relax and take a few deep breaths. In your mind, visualize yourself in the desired outcome scene. You have achieved your outcome. Put yourself fully in the scene and picture it clearly, hear people congratulate you, feel the feelings of accomplishment and pride. Write down each scene in detail. Don't miss any details.

_____

_____

_____

Realm VIII: How will your desired outcome affect your life? What will be added? What will be taken away? Ask yourself, "Am I willing to accept these changes? Am I willing to change my present level of comfort? Am I willing to take the necessary action to facilitate this outcome?" Take your time and write down your answers.

_____

_____

_____

_____

_____

_____

_____

_____

_____

_____

_____

_____

_____

Realm IX. What actions must you take immediately to attain your planned outcome? What are the costs involved? Write down everything.

_____

_____

_____

_____

_____

_____

_____

_____

_____

_____

_____

_____

_____

_____

Realm X. What actions must you take in the future to attain your planned outcome—daily, monthly, yearly? Write it all down.

_____

_____

_____

_____

_____

_____

_____

_____

_____

_____

_____

_____

The Ten Realms of Outcome Planning are a challenge and a stretch. You'll be amazed at how quickly you start to attain your listed outcomes. This process works. Go through it as often as you feel it's necessary. Do it with your spouse to ensure that you are both moving in the same direction. Complete the process with your staff to increase your success rate in business.

A graduate of High Performance, Jim, went through the outcome planning process. He wrote down his desire to write a science fiction novel. This had been a dream for many years, but he had never taken any action to make it happen. Further, Jim wrote down that he'd have a book contract in the next six months. Two weeks after the session, he came to our office on a Friday afternoon with a bottle of champagne in one hand, and a book contract in the other. Outcome planning works!

Remember—no goals, no glory! Surprise yourself. Write down your goals and then stick them in a safe place and look at them in six months or a year. You'll be amazed how many you will have already achieved. In all my research on goal setting I refer back to the Yale study done in the 50s in which a graduating class was surveyed with only three percent of the students having written goals. Twenty years later this same group was surveyed. They were ,making more money than the rest of the class combined. Simply by writing down your goals you increase your chances of achieving them. When you add the other information I've shared with you, you'll be amazed how quickly you get results.

Chapter 12

Passion: The Propelling Force

Nothing great was ever achieved without enthusiasm.
Ralph Waldo Emerson

What's your passion? What makes you happy? What is that one thing that compels you to get out of bed in the morning? What is the one thing that puts a smile on your face and in your heart? It's been said many times, and it is so true. When you do what you love, success will follow. The Ninth Power in the success system is Passion: The Propelling Force.

WHAT IS PASSION?

I have many participants who attend our classes because they feel they have lost their passion, or their focus in life. Others feel they've never really discovered their passion and don't feel enthusiastic.

Maybe you're asking, "What is passion?" As I've said before, as High Performers we reframe things. We've reframed enthusiasm into passion. One of our participants was talking about the difference between enthusiasm and passion and said, "I think of it as if enthusiasm and passion are the same color, with passion a deeper shade of enthusiasm."

Passion is working hard and loving every minute of it. It's running that extra mile, after you're already exhausted. It's falling down ten times and getting up ten times. Passion is a flame that burns inside you with an intensity so strong you can't deny it. It's an intense emotion compelling you to action.

What is passion? I believe passion is love. Love is an uncomfortable emotion for many professionals to think about in terms of creating their success. Think about love and remember the first time you fell in love or the last time you fell in love. You felt so good and so special that you could look at the stapler on your desk and you'd gasp, "Hhhuuuuuhh! What a miracle this stapler is!" This is the same feeling you have to develop for your current job. Love it! Do your absolute best and this very passion will propel you forward.

How will passion help you? When you have true enthusiasm, or passion, for something, anything, it doesn't matter what it is, you automatically want to do it or be involved with it. When you have passion, you become focused and can make everything happen easily.

DEVELOPING YOUR PASSION

How can you develop enthusiasm or passion into your life? How can you become what I call a Passionist? I'll share with you several ways to find and develop your passion.

Always do your best. When you do your best, you develop pride in yourself. Regina, one of our graduates said, "I was told when I started my first job as a dishwasher, I should make the dishes as clean and shiny as I could so I could be proud of my work." This is a good example that no matter what you do, if you do your best, you'll feel good. When you feel good about what you do you develop passion.

Another way to develop passion in yourself is to **share your enthusiasm!** Get people involved in your dream. Tell your friends and family about your dreams. Ask them to support you with positive feedback. Share your enthusiasm about the things that are important to you. You'll find that enthusiasm is contagious. The more you share, the more you get back.

Next, **enhance your skills.** Research tells us we must be retrained every four years, just to keep up with technology. That's how quickly things are changing. It's critical to stay current with today's information. As you increase your abilities you'll gain a fresh outlook on your work, and your life. This will help you be enthusiastic about everything.

One more way to develop your passion is always to **be open to change.** During my ten years at Honeywell, I watched as executives played musical chairs with some out on their ear. I worked through quality circles, quality improvement teams, quality college, and dozens of other programs. I struggled through the implementation of a half dozen computer systems. I watched as the company grew from 300 employees to 2,300 employees. Talk about change! All I could do was hop on the current wave of change and look forward to the renewed excitement it brought every time. I actually looked forward to the next round of excitement. It generated enthusiasm in me to be successful amidst the chaos! I had a manager who put me on every volatile program, because he said I thrived on challenges and made everything turn to gold. You can make things turn to gold if you just ride the wave of change and look forward to the enthusiasm it generates.

Start living your life as if you have **five times more passion.** When you live in the state that you would like to develop, it helps you to become it. The attraction factor takes over our destiny. When we are without passion or enthusiasm, that's what we attract into our lives. When we act five times more passionate, we will become passionate.

Finally, **determine what your passion is**. I've heard a lot of self-help gurus tell us to act enthusiastic and you'll be enthusiastic. I say, "Baloney! If you want to be enthusiastic, you have to find out what makes you feel great and do it!"

FINDING YOUR PASSION

Remember the movie, *City Slickers?* Billy Crystal was told that the meaning to life was just one thing. Find your one thing and you'll always be happy. How do you find your passion or your one thing?

You've got to identify the things that make you smile and feel good when you're doing them. The things that you could do all the time and never get tired of doing them. Then you've found your passion. Here are several steps you can take to determine your passion.

Write down everything you do. Your job, parenting, biking, church, dancing, reading, fishing, anything you can think of. Make sure you cover all the areas of your life including work, play, social, physical, spiritual, and family. Look at each of these items and ask yourself, "When I go to work, am I happy? What parts of my job do I enjoy the most? Do I feel good? Am I pleasant while I am doing it?" Let's face it, if it's a drudge to get out of bed in the morning and go to work, it's not your passion. Do this with each of the items that you wrote down.

Identifying the items you do consistently and asking these questions will help you to know what makes you enthusiastic. We've had lots of people who've completed our training and changed careers. One woman worked for IBM. After our training she decided she'd rather be a photographer. Another participant was a furniture stripper who decided he'd rather be a teacher, another was a salesman who decided he'd rather own his own business.

Another way to identify your passion is to write out a script for your funeral. Sounds a little gruesome, but it can be very helpful. Imagine your life has ended. Who came to your funeral? What did they say about you, what did they say that you liked? What did they say made you happy? After you have written the script, look at the patterns and see if there are particular items that identify your passion.

Or simply let other people tell you what they think makes you happy. Ask friends, co-workers, family members, your spouse, or your minister what they think you like. You'll be amazed at the information you receive. Some of it may not help, but other things may really identify something you've denied or ignored.

Sign up for night school. Talk to a counsellor about the fields that interest you. Take a test that is designed to tell you what you are good at. Learning is a wonderful way to open up new ideas and perhaps help you determine what you want out of life.

Look to the people you admire. Are they doing the things in life you want to do?

Go out and experience life. Break away from daily habits which keep you from new experiences. These new experiences can help you determine your passion. Do volunteer work. My friend, Kim, discovered her passion for marketing by doing promotional work for her local art society. She's so passionate about marketing that I hired her as our director of marketing!

Enthusiasm, according to Webster, means possessed by a God. Since it comes from the Greek word *enthios* meaning "the God within," it makes sense. When you have true passion you are a person possessed with love for life!

QUIETING YOUR VOICE OF JUDGMENT

I have a couple of techniques I'd like to share with you to help you develop and hold onto your passion.

The first technique will help you determine what keeps you from achieving your goals and becoming enthusiastic about life. One of my participants hit this one on the head. She said that she has a little voice that always says things like, "You're not good enough," or "You can't do it." We all have a little voice of judgment. This voice keeps us from reaching our potential and holds back our enthusiasm.

You can quiet your voice of judgment. Give it a name like Buster! We like to call our stoppers Buster Busters. Some ways to quiet your Buster is to become aware of him/her. Give your voice a name, I call mine Effie Louise. Make your Buster ridiculous. Project its voice down to your big toe. It's not easy to take something seriously when it comes from your big toe! Put silly music behind the voice. Tell your Buster to STOP, maybe not out loud. Treat your Buster like your computer. When Buster starts acting up, simply hit the delete key on the computer. Here's an exercise to deflate your inner critic. Try this when you won't be interrupted.

Close your eyes and relax. Imagine in front of you a big blackboard. On it are all the negative thoughts and evaluations you have of yourself. Read through the list and see if anything is missing. At the bottom of the blackboard is an eraser and a piece of chalk. Take the eraser and wipe out the whole list, every last word. Take the chalk and write on the board all of your strengths. Take your time, there's no hurry. Sit back and look over the list.

Know that in the weeks and months to come you will be able to remember these strengths whenever you choose. There is one last thing to attend to. If you look over in the shadows to the left of you, you will see your critic or Buster. Notice there is a valve in the top of Buster's head. If you release the valve all of its power will evaporate. Try it. Open the valve. Hear the rush of air as your voice of judgment begins to deflate. Sagging down to the floor, it sinks and disappears. Lean back and know that anytime your inner critic starts to act powerful, you can reach over and release the valve, letting all the hot air out of your critic. You'll become more enthusiastic knowing that you are in charge.

THE WINNER'S CIRCLE

In order to hold onto this feeling of strength and power, try this. This is called the Winner's Circle.

Stand up and close your eyes. Just relax. Are you ready? Now remember a time of total resourcefulness. A time when you felt enthusiastic and happy. Do you have that picture clearly in mind? Imagine a circle on the floor in front of you. Give the circle a color, maybe your favorite color. Take a deep breath and step into the circle. As you step into the circle, say in your mind a code word that represents the power, strength and enthusiasm that you feel. Intensify the feelings. Make the picture bigger, and brighter. Hear the sounds of people congratulating you. Stay in the circle for fifteen to thirty seconds.

Repeat this exercise two or three times, until you have it anchored. What color was your circle? What was your code word? My color is RED and my code word is Absolutely. This is a very powerful way to hold onto your winning feelings and access that sense of total passion.

As a High Performer, you will fuel your passion by working hard and never accepting the word can't. Reaching your goals celebrating and starting over again. Dare to become a Passionist about your life and then hold on—you'll be propelled forward into greater success!

ACTION PAGE

The great aim of education is not knowledge, but ACTION.
-Herbert Spencer

ACTION STEPS
To High Performance

The major benefit I gained from this chapter was:

_____

_____

_____

_____

Based on this benefit, my High Performance Action Plan is:

_____

_____

_____

_____

Why is this action plan important to me?

_____

_____

_____

_____

Chapter 13

Action: The Catalyst to High Performance

Even if you're on the right track, you'll get run over if
you ain't movin'.
Will Rogers

his is it! The tenth power in the success system. You've been
building one power on another; now it's time to take action and
attain success. Action: The Catalyst to High Performance is the
tenth power in the High Performance Success System. How is action
a catalyst to High Performance? Because action is a stimulant, pro-
viding motivation to change. Once you have developed the first nine
powers, you take action naturally. You become part of what I call the
Action Faction.

THE ACTION FACTION

The Action Faction is a group of individuals who take action,
have a sense of urgency, make things happen, and never give up.
This is a very elite group of individuals. Most people tend to put
things off and avoid action. To join the Action Faction simply acti-
vate yourself. Start taking action the same way you would eat an
elephant, one bite at a time. One step leads to another, which leads
to another. When leaving the corporate environment and starting

my own business, it seemed overwhelming. But I broke the job down into small tasks. Developing a vision, creating a name, applying for a business license, ordering business cards, and researching my competition. It didn't take long to become immersed in the action. This action generated enthusiasm, which generated more action.

OVERCOMING PROCRASTINATION

Procrastination, or anti-action, is the greatest action inhibitor. Nearly everyone procrastinates at times, and for many different reasons. Some people put things off because they're seeking perfection. Those people are so concerned with everything being just right they never seem to finish. Another anti-action person is the one who jumps in with both feet, only to lose steam about half way through the project. They lose interest or become overwhelmed. Then there's the individual who always comes up just a little short and never quite finishes. They have a fear of success.

Sometimes a person will procrastinate because they lack self-esteem, communication skills or even interpersonal skills that will help them move forward. That's one reason we worked on these fundamental skills early in the success model. Another reason people put things off is because it isn't their core desire at all. Someone else is pushing them to finish something.

Whatever reason you have for putting things off, it's time to get busy and just do something, anything, to move you toward your goals. Let's review several ways you can start taking action right now.

First. Get to know yourself. What are your core desires? Write out your feelings about what you want to do and why you want to do it. Understand when you procrastinate and see if there are patterns which hold you back.

Second. If you haven't set your goals and planned your outcomes, then you've missed the key step in taking action. You can't take action until you know what you're moving toward, and why you want to.

Third. Break your goals down into smaller action steps so you don't become overwhelmed. Your outcomes should be planned daily, weekly, monthly and yearly.

Fourth. Visualize yourself as if you have already attained the goal. Seeing is believing, creating action.

Fifth. Become a passionist about your goal. Enthusiasm

moves you forward into action and keeps you moving ahead, even when things aren't going well.

Sixth. Look at your successes. You'll feel good about your accomplishments and naturally want to go for more.

Seventh. Surround yourself with other action-oriented people. Distance yourself from people who are going nowhere.

Eighth. Learn to ask and don't stop asking until you get the right answer. Too many times people are afraid to ask causing them to refrain from taking action. When you do ask, ask intelligently. Ask the person who has the answer!

Ninth. Just do it! Go for it! Get goin'!

MANAGING YOURSELF

Like I said earlier, you can't manage time. The best you can ever do is to manage yourself. When you manage yourself, your time falls into place. Here are some tips to help you become more effective daily.

- **Analyze what you do**

- **Consider a time log**

- **Make a list of things to do daily**

- **Set deadlines for yourself and meet them**

- **Learn to say "No"**

- **Get organized—your work area, your use of time**

- **Trim the fat from your workday—**

    Keep standing

    Keep telephone conversations short

    Limit meetings to 30 minutes

    Write short letters

    Work rapidly

    Get rid of clutter

    Use form letters

    Don't dwell on the past

UNDERSTANDING ACTION

There was a salesman walking down a country road. He passed a farmer standing along side his farm. This was a beautiful farm with rolling hills, fields of corn and wheat, tall red barns and a beautiful well-kept home. The salesman stopped and called to the farmer, "What a beautiful piece of land you have! The Lord has sure been good to you!" The farmer looked at the salesman and replied, "Yes the Lord has given me a beautiful piece of land, but you should have seen it *before* he gave it to me!"

Yes, like all of us, the farmer was given a lot of resources, but it was his action that produced that magnificent farm. The farmer had a wonderful sense of satisfaction, knowing it was his action which made his land the beautiful farm it was.

Before I left the corporate world to enter the world of entrepreneurship, I knew I had a passion, a passion for my goal. More than anything I wanted to spread the High Performance Learning System to as many people as possible. I had never owned my own business before, and I didn't have much money saved to get started. But that didn't stop me. I had passion which caused me to take action. I started looking for ways to make my dream become a reality. Everyone told me I was crazy. My friends said I was nuts for leaving my secure job. But that didn't stop me because I had passion that caused me to take action. I looked for the right city to test market the training and I followed my plan. Even when times were tough, I kept moving forward. Because I had passion which caused me to take action. When I wanted to spread the tools and techniques even further by creating this book and a tape set, we ran into more obstacles. But those didn't stop us because we had passion which caused us to take action. Become a passionist about your goals, and you'll take action and succeed.

A famous talkshow host once interviewed three young successful entrepreneurs. Each of them had become millionaires before age thirty-five. When asked why they were so successful, they all pointed to the same reason: Willingness to take risks. Their willingness to take action without knowing the outcome, or having all the information, enabled them to succeed. This is what I've done in order to share the High Performance Success System with you.

It's important to remember that not all actions lead to our immediate outcome, and that's all right. Consider that experts say a torpedo is off target ninety percent of the time, but it doesn't stop just because of that. It continuously corrects itself as it moves toward its target, until it meets its mark. Our image of a torpedo is that it has complete accuracy. However, it's off target ninety percent of the

186

time. It's the final action of the torpedo that makes it appear so accurate.

A lack of action can cause many of problems for you. It's just like the person who is a couch potato, the one whose only exercise is jumping to conclusions. Your body becomes weak and your muscles ache. The lack of action toward your goals can cause a lowering of your self-esteem and even depression. I have a friend from our training who came to us as an unemployed salesman looking for a job. After describing to him what we sell, he said, "I don't want to work for you I need to take your course!" He did just that. Subsequently he started his own business, and is quite successful now. Simply by taking that first step you will begin a wonderful, energizing journey into the Action Faction.

The natural state of action, which is when you advance toward your goals automatically, happens when you have achieved the mental state where you believe you have already achieved your goal. I'm reminded of this natural state when I think of Ghandi's statement, "I am my message." We always have to begin by knowing that we have already arrived.

It has been said that we are human beings, not human doings. In developing an awareness of this, people often go through the nine phases of self-talk to begin personal change. First they may say, "I can't." Then they move into "I might." After that they state, "I should." Moving on they say, "I want to." The next phase is, "I'll try." Next they say, "I can." Then they move to, "I will." And finally they reach the ninth phase which is, "I am." The ninth phase is where we must be. At the "being" level, we are whole, complete and perfect. It is normal to be healthy, strong and energetic. When we are at the "being" level, we naturally take action. How many times have you looked at a project, or anything new you want to accomplish, and started by saying to yourself, "I can't do this!" Remember what Henry Ford said. "If you think you can, or you think you can't, you're right."

THE "BUT" LADDER

Unfortunately, I hear people make comments all the time such as, "I should have started my own business, but—," "I should start exercising, but—," "I should stop smoking, but—," We've got to stop "shoulding" on ourselves!

You must realize that no action can be taken, nor any goals achieved, until you stop hiding behind all those "BUTS!" I'm going to share a technique with you that will help you get your buts out of the way of taking action.

You'll need some paper and a pen. Use the diagram on the next

187

page. In the circle, write one of your goals. Just a few words. Looking at your goal, think of everything that has kept you from achieving this goal. "I'd start my own business, but I don't have the experience," "I'd start my own business, but I don't have enough money." Push yourself to list every but that has been keeping you from achieving this goal.

Identifying and putting pen to paper as you write out your "buts" is a powerful tool to get you off dead center. As you identify and write out your "buts" you will—

- **understand your fears and let them go.**
- **identify the obstacles in your way.**
- **destroy the power of your obstacles.**
- **gain power because you have taken control.**
- **define a clear plan for your goals.**
- **develop confidence by realizing that your obstacles can be overcome.**

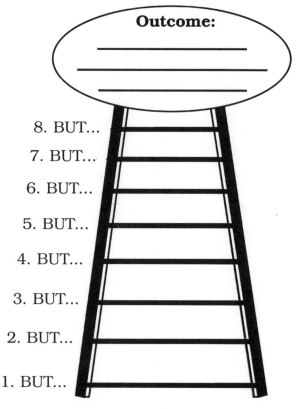

THE RESOURCE LADDER

After you have completed the "BUT" ladder exercise, you have another exercise to complete. This is called a Resource Ladder. Use the diagram on the following page repeating the previous exercise for the "BUT" ladder. This time you fill in the ladder with all the personal resources you have which will help you achieve your goal. Start with the bottom rung, work your way to the top until you have reached your goal. Write in such resources as, I have a friend who can help, or I can borrow the money I need. When you fill in your resource ladder you will:

- **identify all of your resources, some that you may have been overlooking.**

- **become rejuvenated and enthused about attaining your goal.**

- **gain confidence by seeing every resource you have to move you forward.**

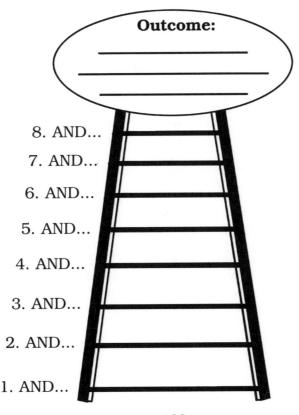

Outcome:

8. AND...
7. AND...
6. AND...
5. AND...
4. AND...
3. AND...
2. AND...
1. AND...

THE GOLD ACTION CARD SYSTEM

Now that you have defined your goals and gained many valuable tools and techniques, you can use this final tool, the High Performance Gold Card System. In our training, at the end of each weekly session, we have participants fill out what we call a Gold Card. This is a three-by-five card—gold of course, because gold is an action color. On this card are the following questions or statements to be answered.

- **My desired outcome for this week is: (write down your goal for the week. What do you want to accomplish? This could be something that you'd like to do, based on your longer range goals. This statement is important because it gives you a clear plan for the week. When you know what you are working on, it's easier to take action.)**

- **Why this outcome is important to me: (Why do you want to achieve this during the next week? Will it keep you on track to a bigger goal? Will it help you become better at something? Understanding why something is important to you will give you a reason to start taking action. It will keep you moving toward your goal.)**

- **My action plan is: (What is your action plan? What steps will you take? What do you need to do to accomplish your desired outcome? Writing out a plan will help keep you on track during the week when you get busy. Remember, plan your work and work your plan.**

- **The High Performance Tools I will use are: (What High Performance Tools will you use to help achieve your goal? Is there a specific tool that will make things happen or make things easier for you? This is a good way to ensure you'll remember to use the tools and practice them. When you use the tools, you become more productive and effective.)**

This Gold Card System (to order call 800-383-6919) is an excellent way for you to make sure you'll use the High Performance Tools. After you have completed your card, keep it with you all the week. Place it wherever you'll see it frequently. This will help make sure you remember to use the tools, and take action toward your goals. Maybe you'll want to keep it in your daily planner or on your bathroom mirror or even on the visor in your car or taped on your desk at work. Keep it close to you for a constant reminder.

After you have accomplished your outcome for the week, keep the gold card in a file box or folder. You will be able to look back through the gold cards and see how much you have accomplished later. Seeing the results you're making helps you develop even more passion, creating even more action.

As a bonus to the gold card system, set up a system of rewards for yourself. Every time you complete your action plan, give yourself a reward. For instance, if you are wanting to eat healthier and you've managed to avoid junk food all week, give yourself a reward. Maybe a movie, a round of golf, or a new piece of clothing you've been wanting.

NEVER GIVE UP

Coach Valvano said, "Don't give up. Don't ever give up." This was just before his death. I think those are words to live by. It's easier to be determined when you are inspired to do so. I've compiled a list of inspiring quotes to help motivate you to never give up—

He conquers who endures.
Persius

Always at it wins the day.
Proverb

Great works are performed not by strength, but
perseverance.
Dr. Johnson

Let me tell you the secret that has led me to my goals.
My strength lies solely in my tenacity

Louis Pasteur

Nothing great was ever done without much enduring.
Saint Catherine of Siena

*When you get into a tight place and everything
goes against you, 'til it seems you could not
hold on a minute longer, never give up then for
that is just the place and time that the tide will
turn.*
Harriet Beecher Stowe

Fall seven times, stand up eight.
Japanese Proverb

*The difference between the impossible and the possible
lies in a person's determination.*
Tommy LaSorda

You're never a loser until you quit trying.
Mike Ditka

When I say never give up, I mean until you have a good reason to
give up. I've witnessed business owners continue a business that
made them absolutely no profit, and made them miserable. If you
analyze things, you'll know when it's the right time to give up.
Remember the preacher who stayed with his church and died even
after he was sent help!

When I think of action I am always reminded of a particular story:

> *This is a story about a family who lived at the top of
> Mount Morgan in Queensland, Australia. Three genera-
> tions of this family had lived on top of this mountain.
> Each family struggled financially, doing everything
> they could to survive. Unfortunately no one was able to
> grow anything on the mountain. The third and final
> family gave up, broken and impoverished. They gave
> in selling their home atop the mountain to another fam-
> ily. Just six months later, the new family discovered
> the richest gold deposit in the world. It was right under
> their home, atop the mountain. It wasn't so bad that
> the other family left their home in total poverty. The
> real tragedy was that the other family had been told
> many years ago that the gold deposit might exist.*

Which family are you like, the first or the second? I challenge you
to be like the second family and take action. When you do, you will
find your gold deposit and become part of the action faction.

192

ACTION PAGE

The great aim of education is not knowledge, but ACTION.
-Herbert Spencer

ACTION STEPS
To High Performance

The major benefit I gained from this chapter was:

_____

_____

_____

_____

Based on this benefit, my High Performance Action Plan is:

_____

_____

_____

_____

Why is this action plan important to me?

_____

_____

_____

_____

Section 5

The Continuation

"The prolonging or extension of your success."

Chapter 14

Working the Success System

Life is what we make it, always has been,
always will be.
Grandma Moses

Working the Success System is an ongoing process. Knowing and understanding the Ten Super Powers of Achievement is only the beginning. Now it's up to you to use the tools and live by the principles I've laid out for you in this book.

Remember that as human beings we are a system. A complex system of cells, nerves, and organic matter. Because of this interdependence we are greater than the sum of our parts. Just like the success system. In our universe, a system can only exist within another system.

It would be very easy to read this book, set it aside and continue with your current behavior. High performance comes only to those who work for it. So, let's look at several ways you can continue to use this system and keep it working for you.

One of my clients told me that when he started the system he was a student. By the time he finished it, he was a teacher. Each day, teach the tools and principles from this system to everyone you meet. Teach them to family, friends and co-workers. Always look for opportunities to share the information with others. Every time you share the information from this success system you reinforce it for yourself. Sharing the tools will make it part of your everyday life.

Some friends of mine learned the system and shared it with their son, who is on the high school swim team. He focused on the outcome planning techniques. He put his goals all over the walls of his room. He visualized the lap time he needed to achieve to qualify for the state tournament. And it happened! As he came up out of the water during that qualifying lap he knew he'd done something he had never done before. He knew he had achieved his goal, even before he had looked at the time clock. Imagine the feeling his parents had knowing they had helped him harness his own mind power to succeed!

Continue to use the tools yourself. When you plan your outcomes and write out your action plan weekly, make sure you write down which tools and principles you're going to use to achieve your outcomes that week. The key to success is knowing and using the tools and principles. None of these techniques will work if you don't use them.

The next way to keep High Performance alive and well daily is to continue building your positive attitude.

Hang around positive people. Avoid the. Another way to maintain your positive attitude is, watch for what people do right! Watch the people around you, your family, friends and co-workers. Challenge yourself to look for the things they do right, and then tell them! Use the complimenting tool and share. You can also maintain your positive attitude by developing your own Success Network. Set up a network of positive High Performers and meet with them regularly, once a month or once a week. Meet and share positives with each other. Teach the tools, and practice them with your network, really become an expert at each technique. Continuously bring new people into your network who can add new ideas bringing more information. Our company has developed a network of positive people who are graduates of the High Performance Training Course. The group is called the Champions Network. Once a month we meet for breakfast or lunch to share positives, and network our businesses. Not only is it good for developing business, but it's a wonderful way to reinforce the success system in yourself.

As Stephanie Luethehans says, "Having it all doesn't mean having it all at once." Revolutionizing yourself is like eating an elephant. Take it one bite at a time!

Finally, to maintain the High Performance way of life, I encourage you to read this book over and over again. Each time you read it, focus on a different area of your life. The more you read, the more you will remember and use. Read and go through the exercises again. It will make a difference in your level of understanding.

Another way to enhance the High Performance process is to keep the High Performance principles and techniques in front of you at all times. There are posters available that will serve as a reminder, and an inspiration, to continue using the information in the system. Encourage your family and co-workers to read this book. You can all benefit from the High Performance tools together.

As you are working the system, it's important to continue to use your owner's manual for your brain, to access more of its unlimited power.

SUMMARY OF SUPER POWERS

I'll summarize all the powers and some tools I've shared throughout this book, to help you remember the essentials of each of the ten super powers of achievement.

Power 1. SELF-ESTEEM—The Foundation of Success

If you have taken the time to make your "I am" tape and listen to it every day, you've already broken through the major barrier to your success, your limiting self-beliefs. Make a daily habit of stating positive affirmations, not only to yourself, but also to others in the form of sincere compliments.

Power 2. COMMUNICATION—The Ultimate Advantage

By using the important information I shared with you from Neurolinguistic Programming, you'll be able to automatically identify the communication styles of everyone around you. Whether their primary style is, visual, auditory, or kinesthetic. What communication style is your spouse? Your boss? Your children? How can you give them information in ways which will help them better understand and act on what you say? I shared with you some tips on public speaking. Always remember to leave your audience with a DUBACUZ...(what you want them to do, because of what they will gain.) This will move your audience to action!

Power 3. HUMAN RELATION SKILLS—The Human Factor

In this section I shared the conversation stack. Met anyone new and tried it out? How about the mirroring and matching? Remember, people like people who are like them. And of course, Geometric Psychology. Are you a triangle, box, circle, or the squiggly line?

Develop each of these personalities styles in yourself and you'll increase your interpersonal skills many times over.

Power 4. POSITIVE ATTITUDE—A Personal Empowerment Model

Your most valuable asset! Did you strike a positive mental attitude yet? Did you ATTITUDINIZE? It's a powerful feeling. Remember to avoid the NIOP's; spend time around positive people only. Even if you must deal with negative people, remember that your positive attitude can have a transforming effect on all those around you.

Power 5. PEACE OF MIND—The High Performance State

Have you experimented with, or used, the Cook's Hook-up? This is one of the most valuable tools you'll ever have. Anytime you're stressed and need to calm down, use the Cook's Hook-up. Your stress will melt away. And—don't sweat the small stuff!

Power 6. PERSONAL BALANCE—Controlling Your World

It all starts within you. The more you understand the connection between your body, mind and spirit, the more you'll be able to balance the power of all three for greater success. Practice working with the three natural laws and you'll enhance your ability to become a High Performer.

Power 7. CREATIVITY—The Whole Brain Adventure

What have you done to switch on your whole brain today? Did you take a different route to work? Done any of the whole brain exercises like the cross crawl

200

or the lazy 8's? Do the switching on techniques before you do Mind Mapping®; you'll generate even more ideas/answers. Switching on your whole brain not only enhances creativity, it makes you much more effective and productive.

Power 8. GOAL SETTING—The Ten Realms of Outcome Planning

I hope you've gone through this exercise at least once alone, and once with your spouse or significant other. When you plan your outcomes and follow the SMART method, Specific, Measurable, Action-oriented, Realistic and True, you begin achieving your goals immediately.

Power 9. PASSION—The Propelling Force

Are you living five times more enthusiastically? Have you looked at what makes you happy, what makes you feel great? When you identify the one thing in life that really gets you excited you will become a passionist about your goals.

Power 10. ACTION—The Catalyst to High Performance

Have you started to take action naturally? Did you get your 'buts' out of the way, and order your gold cards for keeping you on target? If you have planned your outcomes, you will automatically begin to take action. You will become part of the ACTION FACTION.

Congratulations! You've gone through the entire program. You've learned the tools and principles for High Performance Success. You might be thinking, I don't know if these things will really work for me? Let me share with you the story of two individuals who learned this system and used the techniques. Then you can decide.

A woman working in a large corporation learned the tools from the High Performance Success System. She diligently applied them to her job and lived the principles every day. She used the techniques to help her apply for various positions within her organization.

To her amazement, she earned three promotions in eighteen months, increasing her salary by ten thousand dollars a year.

A man working for a large corporation decided it was time to change jobs. He learned the High Performance Success System, and used the tools every day in his job search. At his final interview, he knew he had approximately thirty seconds to make a strong positive impression on the president of the company. He used the mirroring and matching and other rapport building skills. The result was a new position with more prestige. He received a five-thousand-dollar signing bonus and a forty-one percent increase in pay.

These are stories about two, and they are typical of the results we see from those who learn, and use, this system. These two people are no different from you. When you use the tools and principles you'll see amazing results right away. And by the way, the two people I just wrote about are myself and my husband Tom. If we can do it, you can do it!

The world today is moving and changing faster than ever before. We can't succeed by doing "business as usual." Surviving and succeeding throughout the 90s and beyond will require the tools of self-empowerment, the Ten Super Powers of Achievement. You have a great purpose to fulfill, one that will have a larger impact than you can imagine on your company, your community, the country and the world. It all begins with you and your commitment to become a High Performer. Congratulations...you're revolutionized. As Henry Winkler says, A human being's first responsibility is to shake hands with himself. So, shake hands and get going!

To close this book I'd like to share with you a very special story from our training:

There was a wise old woman who lived far up in the mountains. Her wisdom was know far and wide. Two young boys decided to challenge the old woman's wisdom. The boys picked up a bird and started walking the many miles to her cabin. When they arrived, the old woman came out and asked what they wanted. One boy stepped forward, "We want you to tell us if this bird in our hands is alive or dead?" The wise old woman thought for a short time.

Then she looked down at the boys and replied, "If I tell you that the bird in your hands is dead, you will open your hands and show me that it is alive. And if I tell you that the bird in your hands is alive, you'll SMASH it and show me that it is dead. What I would say to you young men is that you have the fate of that bird in your hands."

You have your fate in your hands. I've shared the tools and techniques with you, now you must use them to attain the success you want. Congratulations—You're a High Performer!

AFTERWORD

Revolutionizing yourself is simple but it isn't easy! As I write these final pages of this book, I am forced into a change. I am suddenly separated from my husband, facing imminent divorce. Once again, I must rethink my goals. I must revolutionize myself again to face this new cycle of change. The good news is, I have the tools to do just that!

Friends, prepare yourselves for whatever life throws your way. It isn't easy, but it's worth it in the long run. Flexibility and hardiness are critical. Many will fail to use the tools and refuse to learn. Not everyone will be able to revolutionize. Not everyone will be able to make this giant leap—only the **HIGH PERFORMANCE CHAMPIONS!**

APPENDIX A—Answers

Answers to Brain Aerobics A (page 155)

1. Lying in wait
2. Tally ho
3. Love at first sight
4. Put it in writing
5. Circular reasoning
6. Broken nose
7. A step backward
8. Sold down the river
9. Unfinished symphony
10. Close encounters
11. Outnumbered 3 to 1
12. Odds are against you
13. Raised eybrows
14. Railroad crossing
15. No U Turn
16. Balanced budget

Answers to Brain Aerobics B (page 156)

1. First person singular
2. Add insult to injury
3. Elevator out of order
4. Cubed steak
5. No two ways about it
6. It's a small world after all
7. The odds are overwhelming
8. High seas
9. Getting it all together
10. Jai alai
11. A break in custom
12. Mad about you
13. Teetotaler
14. Singing in the rain
15. The good, the bad, the ugly
16. Call it a day

Count the F's (page 74)

Answer: 6

Answers to Nine Dots A (page 157)

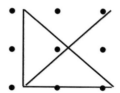

Answers to Nine Dots B (page 157)

Answer 1: Fold the paper so the three lines of dots align closely. Then a single (wide) pencil line will touch all nine dots simultaneously.

Answer 2: Another approach is to use a wide paint brush and with one stroke you'll connect all nine dots at once.

APPENDIX B—THE HIGH PERFORMANCE GLOSSARY OF TERMS

Revolutionize - effect an extreme change in.

VAK - acronym for communication styles, visual, auditory and kinesthetic.

Switching-on - a technique from Educational Kinesiology for involving the whole brain.

NLP - acronym for neurolinguistic programming, a technology for personal change.

EK - acronym for educational kinesiology, a technology for whole brain learning.

NIOP's - acronym for the, negative input of other people.

Action Faction - a High Performer who takes action and makes things happen in a consistent and timely manner.

Attitudinize - to strike or assume a positive mental attitude.

High Performer - one who carries out a consistent, elevated level of performance.

Outcome Planning - the act of formulating a set of actions to achieve a desired result.

Passionist - an individual with intense emotion, zeal or enthusiasm for their desired outcomes.

Personal Balance - the interaction between body, mind and spirit causing stability, equality and harmonious form.

Personal Power - internal strength, courage and savvy.

Stress Captain - an individual with the authority and ability to master the strains in their life and achieve peace of mind.

APPENDIX C—CHARACTER TRAITS

Accessible
Accomplished
Accountable
Accurate
Achiever
Active
Actualizer
Adaptable
Adaptive
Adept
Administrator
Adventurous
Advisor
Affectionate
Affluent
Agreeable
Alert
Altruistic
Ambitious
Amiable
Animated
Appreciative
Approving
Articulate
Artistic
Aspiring
Assertive
Assimilator
Assured
Athletic
Attentive
Attractive
Authentic

Balanced
Believable
Big-hearted
Bold
Boundless
Brave
Bright
Brilliant
Builder
Businesslike

Calm
Candid
Capable
Careful
Caring
Cautious
Centered
Certain
Challenging
Charisma
Charitable
Charming
Cheerful
Childlike
Classy
Clever
Commanding
Commendable
Committed
Compassionate
Compelling
Competent
Competitive
Composed
Compromiser
Concentrated
Concrete
Confident
Congenial
Congruent
Connoisseur
Conscientious
Considerate
Consoler
Consultant
Contented
Controlled
Convincing
Cooperative
Cordial
Courageous
Courteous
Creative
Credible

Creditworthy
Cultured
Curious

Daring
Decisive
Dedicated
Deep thinker
Delightful
Dependable
Determined
Devoted
Dexterous
Diligent
Direct
Distinctive
Distinguished
Doer
Dramatic
Driven
Dynamic

Eager
Earnest
Effective
Efficient
Elegant
Eloquent
Empathetic
Encouraging
Enduring
Energetic
Enterprising
Entertaining
Enthusiastic
Entrepreneurial
Exciting
Exhilarating
Expedient
Experienced
Expert
Explicit

Faithful
Fascinating
Fast
Fastidious
Fearless
Fighter
Finisher
Flexible
Flowing
Focused
Forgiving
Frank
Free-spirited
Friendly
Fun-loving

Generous
Gentle
Genuine
Gifted
Giving
Good communicator
Good judgment
Good memory
Graceful
Gracious
Gregarious

Happy
Hard-working
Harmonious
Health-conscious
Hearty
Helpful
High-spirited
Honest
Honorable
Hopeful
Humble

Idealistic
Imaginative

Impartial
Independent
Individualistic
Industrious
Infallible
Influential
Innocent
Innovative
Insightful
Inspiring
Integrity
Intelligent
Intense
Interesting
Intriguing
Inventive

Jovial
Joyful

Kind
Knowledgeable

Leader
Like able
Limitless
Listener
Lively
Loving
Loyal

Matter-of-fact
Mature
Methodical
Mindful
Motivated
Motivator
Mover

Natural
Noble
Nonjudgmental
Nurturing

Observant
Open-minded

Opportunist
Optimistic
Organized
Original
Outgoing
Outrageous

Patient
Peaceful
Perceptive
Persevering
Persistent
Personable
Pioneer
Playful
Pleasant
Pleasing
Poised
Polite
Popular
Positive
Powerful
Practical
Precise
Prepared
Proud
Principled
Problem-solver
Productive
Professional
Profound
Progressive
Promoter
Prompt
Prosperous
Punctual
Purposeful

Qualified
Quality-con-
  scious
Questioning
Quick
Quick-witted
Radiant
Rational

Real
Realistic
Reasonable
Receptive
Regal
Relaxed
Reliable
Reputable
Resilient
Resolute
Resourceful
Respectable
Respectful
Resplendent
Responsible
Responsive
Restrained
Risk-taker

Secure
Seeking
Self-actualized
Self-confident
Self-controlled
Self-directed
Self-disci-
  plined
Self-reliant
Self-starter
Self-sufficient
Selfless
Sensational
Sense of
  humor
Sensible
Sensitive
Serious
Settled
Sincere
Skillful
Smart
Smiling
Spirited
Stable
Steady
Stimulating

Strong
Successful
Succinct
Supportive
Sure
Sympathetic
Synthesizer
Systematic
Talented
Tender
Thoughtful
Thorough
Tolerant
Tranquil
True
Trustworthy
Tnuthful

Understanding
Unique
Unlimited

Valiant
Versatile
Vibrant
Victorious
Visionary

Warm
Well-rounded
Willing
Winner
Wise
Worker

Young-at-heart
Youthful

Zealous
Zestful

APPENDIX D—RECOMMENDED BOOK LIST

Anthony, Robert, Robert, Ph.D.:
Total Self Confidence

Bach, Richard: *Illusions,
Jonathan Livingston Seagull*

Bandler, Richard: *Using Your
Brain for a Change*

Bandler, Richard & Grinder,
John: *Frogs into Princes*

Benis, Warren & Nanus, Burt:
Leaders

Benson, Herbert, M.D.: *The
Relaxation Response*

Bettger, Frank: *How I Raised
Myself from Failure to Success
in Selling*

Bristol, Claude M.: *The Magic of
Believing*

Bry, Adelaide: *Visualization*

Buscaglia, Leo, Ph.D.: *Living,
Loving & Learning Love,
The Way of the Bull*

Crum, Thomas: *The Magic of
Conflict*

Danforth, William H.: *I Dare You*

Dyer, Wayne, Ph.D.: *Gifts from
Eykis
The Sky's the Limit
Pulling your Own Strings
What do you Really Want for
your Children?
Your Erroneous Zones*

Frankl, Victor: *Man's Search for
Meaning*

Gavin, Shakti: *Creative
Visualization
Living in the Light*

Heider, John: *The Tao of
Leadership*

Hesse, Hermann: *Siddhartha*

Hill, Napoleon: *Think and Grow
Rich*

Hopkins, Tom: *How to Master the
Art of Selling*

Houston, Jean, Ph.D.: *The
Possible Human*

Hubbard, Elbert: *A Message to
Garcia*

Jampolsky, Gerald G., M.D.:
Love is Letting Go of Fear

Kennedy, Danielle: *Super Natural
Selling*

Keyes, Ken: *Handbook to Higher
Consciousness*

Laborde, Genie, Ph.D.:
Influencing with Integrity

Malts, Maxwell, M.D.: *Creative
Living for Today
Psycho-cybernetics*

Mandino, Og: *The Greatest
Miracle in the World
The Greatest Salesman in the
World
The Greatest Secret in the
World*

Mansky, F.A., Jr.: *Secrets of
Effective Leadership*

Millman, Dan: *Way of the
Peaceful Warrior*

Maine, Donald J. & Herd, John
H.: *Modern Persuasion
Strategies*

Murphy, Joseph, Ph.D.: *The
Power of Your Subconscious
Mind*

Patton, Forrest H.: *The
Psychology of Closing Sales*

Peale, Norman Vincent:
*Positive Imaging
The Power of Positive Thinking*

Peters, Tom: *Passion for
Excellence
Thriving on Chaos*

Pirsig, Robert M: *Zen and the Art of Motorcycle Maintenance*
Rand, Ayn:
  Atlas Shrugged
  The Fountainhead
Saint Exupery, Antoine de:*The Little Prince*
Satir, Virginia: *Peoplemaking*
Schuller, Robert, D.D.: *Self-Love, The Be Happy Attitudes, Tough Times Never Last, Tough People Do*
Schwartz, David J.: *The Magic of Thinking Big*
Sculley, John:*Odyssey*
Wonder, Jacquelyn & Donovan, Priscilla:*Whole-Brain Thinking*
Von Oech, Roger, Ph.D.:*A Whack on the Side of the Head*
Zdenek, Marilee:*The Right Brain Experience*

APPENDIX E—SUGGESTED AUDIO TAPES

Dr. Robert Anthony
  Beyond Positive Thinking
  Communicate with Self-Confidence

Leo Buscaglia
  Loving Each Other

Roger Damson
  The Secrets of Power Negotiating
  You Can Make Your Life an Adventure

Dr. Wayne Dyer
  How to Be a No-Limit Person
  Secrets of the Universe
  Transformation: You'll See it When You Believe It
  What Do You Really Want for Your Children?

Jerry Billies
  Money Love

Dr. Jerry Jampolsky
  Love is Letting Go of Fear

Tom Peters
  The New Masters of Excellence
  Thriving on Chaos

Hugh Prather
  How to Live in the World and Still Be Happy

Anthony Bobbins
  Unlimited Power

Jim Rohn
  Success Strategies

Brian Tracy
  Secrets of Success of Self-Made Millionaires
  The Psychology of Achievement
  The Psychology of Selling
  The Psychology of Success

Denis E. Waitley
  Seeds of Greatness
  The Inner Winner
  The Psychology of Winning

Zig Ziglar
  See you at the Top

Bibliography

Abrecht, Karl. *Brain Power: Learn to Improve Your Thinking Skills.* New Jersey: Prentice Hall Press, 1980.

Austin, Diane, and Don Aspromonte. *Green Light Selling.* Colorado: Cahill Mountain Press, Incorporated, 1990.

Blanchard, Kenneth, Ph.D., and Donald Carew, Ph.D., Eunice Parisi-Carew, Ed.D. *The One Minute Manager Builds High Performing Teams.* William Morrow and Company, Incorporated, 1990.

Bloomfield, Harold H., Ph.D., et al. *TM: Discovering Inner Energy and Overcoming Stress.* New York: Dell Publishing Company, Incorporated, 1975.

Branden, Nathaniel. *Honoring the Self.* New York: Bantam Books, 1983.

Brooks, Michael. *Instant Rapport.* Warner Books, 1990.

Buzan, Tony. *Use Both Sides of Your Brain.* Plume, 1991, third edition.

Dellinger, Susan, Ph.D. *Psycho-Geometrics: How to Use Geometric Psychology to Influence People.* New Jersey: Prentice Hall Press, 1989.

Dennison, Paul, Ph.D. and Gail E. Dennison. *Brain Gym.* California: Edu-Kinesthetics, Incorporated, 1989.

Korda, Michael. *Power.* New York: Random House, 1975.

Kushner, Malcolm. *The Light Touch: How to Use Humor for Business Success.* New York: Simon and Schuster, 1990.

LeBoeuf, Michael, Ph.D. *Imagineering: How to Profit From Your Creative Powers.* New York: Berkley Books, 1980.

Lewis, Phillip V., *Organizational Communication: The Essence of Effective Management,* 2nd ed. Columbus, Ohio: Grid, 1980.

Mayer, Jeffery J. *If You Haven't Got the Time to Do It Right, When Will You Find the Time to Do It Over?* New York: Simon and Schuster, 1990.

McCay, James T. *The Management of Time.* New Jersey: Prentice Hall, Incorporated, 1979.

Millman, Dan. *The Warrior Athlete: Body, Mind, and Spirit.* New York: Stillpoint Publishing, 1979.

Osborn, Alex, L.H.D. *Applied Imagination.* 3rd ed. New York: Charles Scribner's Sons, 1963.

Owen, Keith Q. and Barbara P. Mink, Oscar G. Mink. *Groups at Work.* New Jersey: Educational Technology Publications, 1987.

Rinzler, Alan and Michael Ray. *The New Paradigm in Business.* New York: World Business Academy, 1993.

Shone, Ronald. *Creative Visualization: How to Use Imagination for Self Improvement.* Vermont: Destiny Books, 1988.

Suid, Murray and Wanda Lincoln. *The Teacher's Quotation Book - Little Lessons On Learning.* Dale Seymour Publications, 1986.

Trimm, Paul R. *Managerial Commuinication: A Finger on the Pulse.* 2nd ed. New Jersey: Prentice Hall, 1986.

Wycoff, Joyce, *Mindmapping®,* Berkley, 1991

INDEX

ORDER FORM

ITEM	QTY.	PRICE	TOTAL
Revolutionize Yourself, book	_____	$12.95 ea	_____
The High Performance Success System: 10 Super Powers of Achievement, audio tape set, includes six audio cassettes featuring twelve individual sessions, and a sixteen page workbook in a sturdy vinyl case.	_____	$59.95 ea	
Gold Card Action System	_____	$3.95 ea	_____
Biodots with Directions	_____	$2.00/5 dots	_____
Missouri Tax		6.975%	_____
Shipping/Handling - Tape set		$3.95	_____
Shipping/Handling - Book		$1.75	_____
TOTAL ORDER			_____

(If you order more than one item, call (800) 383-6919 for the shipping/handling charges)

Ship To—

_____
Name

_____
Address   City   State   Zip

_____
Telephone

Form of payment:
       ❑ **Check/Moneyorder enclosed**
       ❑ **Bill my VISA/MC**

_____
Number   Expiration Date

_____
Name as appears on card (PRINT)

_____
Signature

To order with your VISA/MC by phone, call (314) 442-0077 locally or (800) 383-6919 outside Columbia. FAX your order and bill to your VISA/MC (314) 874-7019. Or mail your check to **Innovative Training Systems**, 1301 Vandiver Dr., Suite 100, Columbia, MO 65202

You can have Cheri come to your organization or company for a seminar or workshop by contacting her at Innovative Training Systems.